From Good Will to Civil Rights

Health, Society, and Policy
a series edited by Sheryl Ruzek and
Irving Kenneth Zola

From Good Will to Civil Rights

Transforming Federal Disability Policy

Richard K. Scotch

Temple University Press
Philadelphia

Temple University Press, Philadelphia 19122
© 1984 by Temple University. All rights reserved
Published 1984
Printed in the United States of America

Library of Congress Cataloging in Publication Data

Scotch, Richard K., 1951–
    From Good Will to Civil Rights.

    (Health, Society, and Policy)
    Includes index.
    1. Handicapped—Legal status, laws, etc.—United States.
2. Handicapped—Government policy—United States.
I. Title.
II. Series.
KF480.S3   1984   346.7301'3   84-8478
ISBN 0-87722-363-7   347.30613

To Leslie

Contents

Acknowledgments

Many, many people contributed to this book. My mother and father served as models of creative inquiry and concern for all kinds of people. My formal training in sociology has built on the strong base they provided. In the course of my research and writing, I received various forms of aid and comfort from Eleanor and David Ayman, Freda and Norman Scotch, Charlotte and Bernard Scotch, Dorian and Melvin Linton, Pat Cox and John Butler, Susan Klinger and Joshua Weiner, and Patricia Asch. The Harvard Sociology Department provided funds for much of my travel and for tape recording equipment.

I first became interested in the role of symbols in social reform as the result of discussions with Joel Levin and with my fellow graduate students in the Harvard Sociology Department. My involvement with the issue of civil rights for disabled people was stimulated by my work with the Virginia Division for Children. Donald Warwick gave particularly helpful counsel on framing research questions, conducting field interviews, and analyzing qualitative data. Valuable comments and suggestions were also given by Ann Swidler, Paul DiMaggio, John Butler, Nathan Glazer, Sheryl Ruzek, and Irving Zola. Janet Francendese of Temple University Press provided considerable insight and encouragement as I revised the manuscript. Cynthia Keheley prepared several drafts with precision and patience.

Over one hundred people were contacted in the course of my research, almost half of whom were formally interviewed. Virtually all of them cooperated en-

Acknowledgments

thusiastically, generously giving their time, their ideas, and a wealth of information. Particular help was provided by Jill Robinson, Ann Rosewater, Richard Sternberg, Ned Stuttman, John Williams, and John Wodatch.

The symbol used on the cover of this book is based on a logo used by Disabled in Action of metropolitan New York and originally designed by Patricio Figueroa. Their permission for its use is gratefully acknowledged.

My largest debt of gratitude is to Leslie Linton. She has been an active participant in all of the work that culminated in this book, contributing creativity, good judgment, intellectual rigor, and the ability to translate academese into intelligible English. She has enriched my work in many ways.

Finally, this book is an acknowledgment of the many advocates, disabled and able-bodied, outside and inside of government, who have worked long and hard to bring down the barriers facing people with disabilities. Only a small portion of their efforts is chronicled here.

From Good Will
to Civil Rights

A Civil Rights Law for Disabled People

During the 1970s, a time of increasing concern about the limits of public resources and governmental action, the federal government issued a mandate that people with physical and mental disabilities must have equal access to programs and activities supported with federal funds.[1] The mandate was unequivocal, without regard to cost or disruption to the recipients of federal funds. Why was such a commitment made? Was it only a well-meaning gesture? Was it the result of political pressure from the disabled community? Was it an isolated effort, or part of some larger public strategy for assisting disabled people?

Section 504 of the Rehabilitation Act of 1973 has been hailed as the first major civil rights legislation for disabled people. In contrast to earlier legislation that provides or extends benefits to disabled persons, it establishes full social participation as a civil right and represents a transformation of federal disability policy. Section 504 prohibits recipients of federal funds from discriminating on the basis of physical or mental handicap and, since its passage, has evolved into a far-reaching guarantee of accessibility to federally funded facilities and programs. To date, the implementation of Section 504 has mandated architectural and service delivery changes that have cost billions of dollars.

Although its importance to millions of Americans is now evident, Section 504 began as an inconspicuous segment of routine legislation.

On September 26, 1973, President Richard M. Nixon

4

signed into law the Rehabilitation Act of 1973, Public Law (P.L.) 93-112. This law provided for the continuation of the vocational rehabilitation program first established by the Smith-Fess Act of 1920, under which federal financial assistance was given to the states for vocational and other services to disabled people. P.L. 93-112 authorized additional funding for the program and provided for a number of new services. At the end of the law was an apparently minor section, Section 504, consisting of one sentence: "No otherwise handicapped individual in the United States, as defined in section 7 (6), shall, solely by reason of his handicap, be excluded from participation in, be denied the benefits of, or be subjected to discrimination under any program or activity receiving Federal financial assistance."

The legislative history of P.L. 93-112 indicates that Section 504 had no special significance at this point in its evolution. The section was not discussed in any of the hearings held prior to the law's passage, nor was it discussed when the bill was considered on the floors of the House and the Senate. There was no public debate on the provision, and the lengthy House and Senate reports on P.L. 93-112 refer only briefly to Section 504:

> The bill further includes a provision proclaiming a policy of nondiscrimination against otherwise qualified handicapped individuals with respect to participation in or access to any program which is in receipt of Federal financial assistance.[2]
>
> Section (504) provides that no otherwise qualified handicapped individual will be discriminated against or excluded from participation in any benefits of any program or activity receiving participation in any benefits of any program or activity receiving Federal assistance.[3]

In the House and Senate reports, the costs estimated for the implementation of P.L. 93-112 include no figures for Section 504, indicating that the bill's authors expected that it would not entail any federal expenditures.

Section 504 was apparently a routine inclusion, a noncontroversial bow toward equal access with no significant commitment of federal authority. In the nine years following the enactment of P.L. 93-112, however, the section has had important effects on many federal programs, including the architecture of buildings housing federally funded programs, the design of urban mass transit systems, the entrance requirements and programs offered in higher education, and the employment requirements for individuals in federally operated and funded projects.

Unlike the statutory provision, the regulations for implementing Section 504 were highly controversial. The first regulation, for programs funded by the Department of Health, Education, and Welfare (HEW), was not issued until four years after passage of the law, and then only after a change of presidential administrations and sit-ins in federal office buildings in Washington and San Francisco. Section 504 regulations for other departments were not published for several additional years.

Why did Congress's brief statement of good intentions create complex problems for regulation? What were the issues that brought masses of disabled people into public forums to demonstrate on behalf of the regulations? Answers to these questions must be sought in the context of a developing civil rights movement and public policy trends.

A Civil Rights Movement

Because of the diverse physical, mental, and emotional conditions included within legal definitions of disability, the disabled population in the United States does not appear to be a cohesive social group. Further, as an aggregation of individuals, disabled people do not share common social positions, common cultural categories, or common interaction patterns. Disabled persons do, however, have exclusion in common. Many disabled people have been excluded from full social participation due to their disabilities, whether because of functional limitations caused by the disabling condition or because of stigmatization. Until fairly recently, this exclusion has impeded them from developing a common identity or literally meeting on common ground. Interaction among disabled people sometimes reflects the stigmatization of disability practiced by the rest of society. In such instances, disabled individuals deliberately distance themselves from each other or make invidious distinctions between good and bad handicaps, rather than seeking to develop social ties on the basis of common experiences and similar social positions.[4]

In recent years, however, a small but growing number of disabled people have created a community both through informal interaction and through formal organizations, first within disability groups such as groups of blind persons or paraplegics and ultimately across disability lines. In the evolution of the disability community, exclusion came to play a positive role. Rather than being a source of negative self-images and a barrier to interaction, the common experience of exclusion became a catalyst for shared identity and a target for collective action. Following in the wake of the black power, feminist, and other social movements of the 1960s, which also stressed a positive self-image rooted in the collective identity of an excluded group demanding greater participation, increasing numbers of disabled people embraced activism and the creation of community. Other factors nurtured a social movement of disabled people by increasing their numbers, their independence, and their dissatisfaction with marginal social participation. These factors include:

- the development of medical technologies, including prosthetics, medications, and surgical techniques, that permit disabled people to live longer, survive injuries, and participate more fully in everyday life;

- the popularizing of an ideology of deinstitutionalization and normalization in mental health and other fields, which encouraged the growth of noninstitutional support systems and greater participation in community life;

- the changing age structure and the increasing number of elderly people in American society, many of whom have physical disabilities or share service needs as well as an activist orientation with disabled persons;

- the Vietnam war, which produced a large number of disabled veterans who were activists, and which also led to widespread protests that helped to legitimate social activism.

The development of a disability community was also encouraged by trends in public policy; as the community grew, it in turn affected those trends.

Public Policy Trends

Section 504 represented the convergence of two trends in public policy: one trend toward extending civil rights protections to groups excluded from full participation in American society and another toward broadening the scope of public programs benefiting disabled individuals.

In the 1970 United States Census, more than 9 percent of the adult population identified themselves as disabled.[5] Despite their large numbers, the disabled population has not been particularly visible to most Americans nor has it generally exhibited the social cohesion or capacity for collective action of an organized community. The large numbers of disabled people in our society have not been visible, and consequently the nature of the real barriers they face has not been well understood. Disabled people generally have not spoken for themselves, and public policies have typically dealt with their needs in ways shaped by stereotypes of dependency.

Beginning in the 1960s, however, government officials and the general public have become increasingly aware of the barriers confronting disabled people, and this awareness has been expressed in public law. At the federal level, a number of major programs have been enacted in the past fifteen years:

8

- The Architectural Barriers Act of 1968 provides for the removal of architectural barriers from new federally-funded buildings. An interagency Architectural and Transportation Barriers Compliance Board was created in 1973 to ensure compliance with the act.

- A number of vocational and independent living services are available under the vocational rehabilitation program. Substantial expansions of the funding of vocational rehabilitation and related services were enacted in 1968, 1973, and 1978.

- A wide range of services is available to individuals with developmental disabilities[6] under the provisions of the Developmental Disabilities Services and Facilities Construction Act of 1970, including day care, medical assistance, special employment and living arrangements, counseling, and recreation. The 1975 amendments to the act funded advocacy agencies to promote the rights of developmentally disabled people.

- Under Title XVI of the Social Security Act, enacted in 1972, direct cash payments are available to disabled people who have limited income and resources. Individuals who are eligible for this program, called Supplemental Security Income (SSI), have also been entitled to food stamps, medical assistance through Medicaid, and a range of social services.

- Since 1974, Project Head Start has been mandated to include disabled children as at least 10 percent of the children enrolled in each program.

- The Education for All Handicapped Children Act of 1974, Public Law 94-142, requires all public school systems to provide a free and appropriate public education and related services to children regardless of handicapping condition, in the least restrictive environment that is appropriate to the individuals.

- Section 504 of the Rehabilitation Act of 1973 declares that no recipient of federal funds may discriminate against any individual in the provision of services, regardless of handicap.

These programs, created or significantly expanded since 1968, were developed within the context of a growing movement among and on behalf of disabled people. To an unprecedented extent, disabled and able-bodied individuals, organizations within various disability groups, coalitions of those organizations, and associations representing service providers combined advocacy efforts to improve social opportunities for disabled people. Although an important objective for these advocacy organizations was increased funding for existing benefits and services, they were dissatisfied with established programs that had been justified by defining disabled individuals as incapable of taking care of themselves and thus in need of special services. Disabled people had been included among the so-called deserving poor—those society considered to be dependent through no fault of their own and therefore entitled to public assistance. Most programs perpetuated an image of disabled people as socially incomplete or damaged as a result of their physical or mental impairments. Seen as incapable of self-sufficiency, they were to be pitied, and stigmatized; both help and segregation were deemed appropriate.[7]

Such views were deeply entrenched in American society. Frank Laski has written of the constraints placed on disabled people by laws that limit the options open to them. Laski, an attorney, has been associated with the Public Interest Law Center of Philadelphia (PILCOP) and was actively involved in litigation to establish the rights of disabled people. He writes that, until very recently, statutes

> reflected common stereotypes of disabled persons as dependent and inferior. Laws characteristically excluded handicapped persons from services, benefits and protections provided, as a matter-of-course, to all persons. Specialized legislation enacted to protect the disabled was premised on notions of charity rather than entitlement and implemented so as to segregate the disabled and suffocate their ability to participate in society.[8]

Some of the disability legislation enacted since the late 1960s strengthened programs that incorporated this dependent image of disabled people. However, other laws mandated an end to the exclusion of disabled people from activities in which their participation had previously been discouraged or prohibited. A wide range of governmental services that had been available only to the able-bodied population was extended statutorily specifically to include disabled people. Advocates argued that disabled people should receive not special education at a special school, but supplemental services as part of a regular educational program in a regular classroom shared with able-bodied students; not sheltered workshops for the construction of handicrafts and the repair of discards, but participation in the mainstream labor market; not separate arrangements for transportation, recreation, and access to public facilities, but equal access to facilities and services used by the general public. By rejecting separate facilities, whether equal or unequal, disability rights advocates rejected the association of disabled persons with the "deserving poor" and launched a civil rights movement demanding full integration into the mainstream of American life, a movement parallel to those demanding equal rights without regard to race, gender, or age.

Like activists in other civil rights movements, activists in the disability rights movement have argued that equal opportunity may require more than simply equal treatment but with a different rationale. Whereas the other movements have justified the need for compensatory efforts primarily as a transitional remedy for past wrongs, most disability rights advocates acknowledge that disabled persons require and will continue to require far more services than able-bodied persons to have truly equal access and equal opportunity. Several of the new federal disability programs, most notably the Education for All Handicapped Children Act and Section 504 of the Rehabilitation Act, provide for substantial compensatory measures. School systems were required to provide for the education of the most severely and profoundly handicapped, at a cost of millions of dollars nationwide. Equal access to transportation under Section 504 was interpreted to require full accessibility for all new public transit buses. Accommodations in the design of transit systems, federal buildings, education institutions, and a number of other facilities and services required tremendous efforts and the commitment of many billions of dollars.

That disabled people could secure such commitments in the fiscally conservative 1970s is surprising. The success of the disability rights movement and its role in the development of Section 504 cannot be explained by the numbers of participants or the degree of their frustration. The lore of social movements and political power offers only partial explanation.

Social Movements and Political Power

In social science the pluralist perspective is the dominant explanation for how interest groups influence public policy.[9] The pluralist perspective explains political effectiveness by concentrating on the political clout of organized interest groups through the use of such resources as money, the mobilization of masses of people in elections or protests, and the dispensing of political favors through occupying strategic political or economic positions. Was an organized movement of disabled people instrumental in transforming federal disability policy? The social movement of disabled people appears atypical of groups that have effectively wielded power in recent American history; the successes of the disability rights movement have not been proportionate to its ability either to exchange favors or to disrupt. Although a sizable proportion of the population describes themselves as having a work-related disability, for most people such self-identification does not translate into group consciousness or political activity and disabled people have not constituted a subculture in our society beyond isolated institutional or community settings. Although disabled people are disproportionately poor, old, and nonwhite, they are geographically and socially dispersed.[10] Severely impaired individuals, who are most likely to identify themselves as "disabled" may face the greatest handicaps to effective public action. Those who are least impaired may choose to reject the disabled label altogether.

Further, disabled people lack many of the political and economic resources typically associated with political influence. As a group they have been unable to mobilize large numbers of people in elections or other collective political or economic activities. To the extent that disabled people do participate in American political and economic life, they typically do so as individuals and often in peripheral positions. The attitudes and behavior of able-bodied people may serve to discourage or explicitly block efforts to attain positions of power. In short, disabled people apparently lack the ability to force institutional change.

An alternative explanation of recent legislation benefiting disabled people characterizes the new mandates as a logical extension of a pattern of expanding entitlements and services provided by the federal government, based on broadly held social and political values—what Daniel Bell has called the Revolution of Rising Entitlements.[11] Civil rights for disabled people could be portrayed as a logical outgrowth of prohibitions to discrimination on the basis of race, ethnicity, sex, and age written into federal legislation and judicial rulings in the last quarter-century. Furthermore, given the periodic expansion of services to disabled people, ensuring equal access to services funded by the federal government in Section 504 would be consistent with the federal government's initiatives in providing opportunities to groups excluded from full social participation.

By emphasizing its continuity with earlier efforts, this cultural/historical approach may help to explain why the cause of civil rights for disabled people was acceptable both in government and among the general public; it cannot, however, explain why the issue was raised at a particular time and place and in a particular way. It cannot explain why these demands were given legitimacy by a government agency in a conservative administration when the very concept of affirmative action programs was increasingly under fire or how effective political action overcomes political conservatism and bureaucratic inertia.

The story of Section 504's institutionalization as a meaningful civil rights protection is complex, involving many individuals and organizations engaged in formal and informal processes. This book traces the stages in

Section 504's evolution—from its origins in legislative proposals to the Rehabilitation Act's passage, to the development of its regulations, through its implementation history. It focuses on a government making policy as well as on a growing community and its struggle for power. It is an attempt to describe and explain a process of policy development in relation to its organizational, political, and historical contexts. The case of Section 504 suggests how symbols, along with a number of organizational and structural factors, can play an important role in public policy. Examining the interplay of these factors may provide a better understanding of how specific policy decisions relate to the broader social forces surrounding them.

14

From Good Will to Civil Rights

In most cultures, disabled people have been supported within the context of the family and the community. In the West, however, as family and community support systems broke down, physically and mentally disabled persons were relegated to custodial institutions. Until the late Middle Ages, they were typically placed in institutions with a variety of other individuals who did not play a productive role in the social and economic life of the community. For the most part, these institutions were supported by religious groups and private benefactors. Virtually all of them took disabled children and adults out of their communities and provided training in isolation from able-bodied persons.

The first separate institutions for disabled persons were asylums for disabled soldiers. One of the earliest asylums was established for blind soldiers in Paris in 1260. Beginning in the sixteenth century, several attempts had been made in Western Europe to establish institutions for the care and training of handicapped children.[1] By the time of the French Revolution, a number of institutions had shown progress in the instruction of deaf, blind, and crippled people. Notable among these was the Institution Nationale, founded in Paris in 1784, where Louis Braille studied and ultimately developed his system of printing for blind persons in 1829.

The first institutions for disabled people in the United States were established in the early nineteenth century. In 1812, a school for blind persons was opened in Baltimore, and in 1817 Thomas Hopkins Gallaudet founded his school for deaf persons in Hartford. Another educational facility, the Perkins Institute and Massachusetts School for the Blind, was established in Boston in 1823. Those private efforts were followed by the establishment of public institutions for mentally and physically disabled persons. In the 1830s, Dorothea Dix led reformers in urging state governments to build public hospitals for mentally ill persons. Dix persuaded Congress to pass a bill providing federal funds for such hospitals, but the legislation was vetoed by President Franklin Pierce on the grounds that such support was not a federal responsibility.

Institutions for disabled persons were founded with great hopes for improving society. In the decades that followed, however, efforts at rehabilitation and social reform proved to be overly optimistic. Institutions took on an essentially custodial nature, overladen with the rhetoric of reform.[2]

The late nineteenth century was a time for many different social reform efforts by nongovernmental voluntary organizations dedicated to serving dependent persons, including disabled persons. Among the earliest such organizations was the Salvation Army, founded in England, which came to the United States in 1879. The American Red Cross was established in 1881, and under its auspices the Red Cross Institute for Crippled and Disabled Men was founded in New York City. The Red Cross also sponsored Braille transcriptions, a service later taken over by the Library of Congress.

This growth of charitable concern for disabled persons continued and expanded in the Progressive Era of the early twentieth century. In 1902, Goodwill Industries was founded by a Methodist minister. Later taken over by the Methodist Board of Missions, Goodwill operated one of the first sheltered workshop programs for physically handicapped persons. A number of other groups were founded in this period, including the Na-

16

tional Tuberculosis Association, the National Association for Mental Health, and the National Easter Seal Society for Crippled Children and Adults, which grew out of the work of local Rotary Clubs in Ohio.

The U.S. Public Health Service

The role of the federal government in providing for the needs of disabled people first took on major importance in the aftermath of the two world wars and the Great Depression. However, there are precedents for federal concern with disabled people that date back to the early days of the nation.

In 1798, in response to concerns about maintaining a strong merchant marine, President John Adams signed into law an act that provided for the relief of sick and disabled sailors. A marine hospital was built in Boston, and services were provided in other major seaports along the east coast. These were supplemented, beginning in the 1830s, by hospitals in ports on the Great Lakes and the Ohio and Mississippi river systems.

By the late nineteenth century, the Marine Hospital Service, which operated these facilities, was also concerned with the control of epidemics of cholera, yellow fever, and other communicable diseases. The service was reorganized in 1902 to become the Public Health and Marine Hospital Service. Later renamed the Public Health Service, this federal agency became involved with the control of food and drugs, the control of disease, emergency health and sanitation, training programs for health care professionals, the construction of health facilities, and several other health-related activities.

The growth in private charity and the transformation of the Public Health Service in the decades around the turn of the century may both be seen as byproducts of the transformation of the United States into an urban in-

17

dustrial society. Two other components of the developing societal response to disability are more directly attributable to the nature of the emerging industrial forms of work. The first is workers' compensation; the second, vocational rehabilitation.

Workers' Compensation

18

The concept that an injured person is entitled to redress by those responsible for the injury is not a product of modern society. It is found in most societies and was enunciated in the earliest recorded legal systems. Under English Common Law, an employer was obligated to assist employees who had been injured on the job. However, the liability of employers came to be substantially limited with the advent of capitalism. Injured employees could not collect damages if they were judged to be negligent, if the injury was caused by another employee, or if the worker was considered to have assumed the risks of a job by accepting the position when dangerous conditions were present. Under these limitations, disabled victims of industrial accidents typically were not compensated.

As industrial work became more mechanized and working conditions were less under the control of workers, there were increasing numbers of injuries in the workplace. Progressive Era reformers reacted to this increase by lobbying for passage of workers' compensation laws, which stipulated compensation for those injured on the job. Although the earliest state laws passed in 1909 and 1910 were ruled unconstitutional, by 1921 forty-five states and territories had passed legislation establishing workers' compensation. These laws usually provided for both medical treatment and financial compensation for injured workers. This type of compensation was similar to compensations already being provided to disabled military veterans. Since the Revolutionary War, disabled veterans had been receiving benefits such as medical care, pensions, sheltered "homes," and land grants.

The Federal Vocational Rehabilitation Program

Since a basic element in the industrialization of the American economy was a supply of skilled and semi-skilled labor, progressive educators who were concerned with the relationship of schooling to adult life developed vocational education programs within the rapidly expanding public school systems of the early twentieth century.[3] Accompanying vocational training programs were vocational guidance counselors, who helped to channel students into various types of training based on assessment of individual aptitudes. Vocational guidance became an established profession; by 1913, the National Vocational Guidance Association was formed. A related field, industrial psychology, employed many of the same techniques in assisting industry in allocating, structuring, and controlling its workforce.[4] A significant contribution to these fields was the development by Alfred Binet of tests purporting to measure intelligence. These tests were first used widely for placement purposes by the American armed forces in World War I.

The federal government legitimated vocational training and guidance when, just before America's entry into World War I, two laws were passed. The first, the National Defense Act of 1916, provided for vocational education and training for members of the armed forces. The establishment of this program for the military was followed in 1917 by passage of the Smith-Hughes Act, which created vocational training programs for youth migrating from rural to urban areas. The programs were to be operated by state departments of education, par-

19

tially funded by the federal government, and administered by a newly created Federal Board for Vocational Education. Both of these laws recognized the importance of vocational training and guidance. They were followed by the first statute which mandated rehabilitation for disabled persons, the Smith-Sears Veterans' Rehabilitation Act of 1918,[5] which established a program of vocational training for disabled veterans. The program was structured in the same way as that set up by the Smith-Hughes Act and was also to be administered by the Federal Board for Vocational Education. Administered by a board already running a civilian program, the Smith-Sears program would prove to be easily adapted into a broader operation in 1920, when Congress established a general vocational rehabilitation (VR) program for disabled citizens under the terms of the Smith-Fess Act.

The Smith-Fess Act of 1920, Public Law 236, was signed into law by President Woodrow Wilson on June 20, 1920. The law authorized limited services for physically handicapped persons, including vocational training, job placement, and counseling. These services were to be provided by state departments of education, with half of the cost assumed by the federal government. Like its two predecessors, the program was to be administered by the Federal Board for Vocational Education. This overall structure of the vocational rehabilitation program has continued to the present, although with major programmatic additions and greater financial responsibility assumed by the federal government.

The initial appropriation for vocational rehabilitation was one million dollars a year, to be matched on a fifty-fifty basis by the states and distributed on the basis of population. Rehabilitation clients were to be at least sixteen years of age, and their disability had to be such that they had the potential for gainful employment, although homemakers were also to be eligible for services.

Within a year and a half after enactment of P.L. 236, thirty-four states had passed laws creating state VR units, although it was not until 1935 that all states had VR programs in operation. The federal statute was periodically reauthorized, with few changes made until the program was incorporated into the New Deal in 1933, when the VR program, along with the Federal Board for Vocational Education, was transferred by executive order to the Office of Education within the Department of the Interior. It was also in 1933 that the first step beyond a program of strictly vocational guidance was made. Living expenses began to be provided to some VR clients, out of an annual appropriation of $840,000 made for this purpose. Since it was the height of the Depression, the program emphasized services to indigent disabled persons.

The program was further strengthened in 1935, with the passage of the Social Security Act. For the first time, the vocational rehabilitation program was given a permanent authorization. Grants to the states were increased to nearly two million dollars annually. Four years later, the vocational rehabilitation program, along with other federal health, education, and welfare agencies, was merged into the new Federal Security Agency. This reorganization included making vocational rehabilitation a separate division of the Office for Education and no longer a subunit of the Vocational Education Division.

In 1940, the program was expanded further. Services were extended to disabled people working in sheltered workshops, to severely disabled people who were homebound, and to disabled individuals in the workforce who required VR services in order to remain employed. Grants to the states were increased another 75 percent, and continued to increase in the early 1940s.

The next major change in the vocational rehabilitation program took place in 1943, as part of the overall war effort in civilian industry. Public Law 113, the Barden-LaFollette Act of 1943, provided federal funds for a number of medical and reconstructive services that had not previously been provided under vocational rehabilitation. For the first time the 1943 act also defined as disabled individuals who were mentally ill or mentally retarded. Through the act, Congress sought to channel disabled workers into war production and to develop comprehensive services for disabled civilians, with an eye toward the disabled military personnel who would be re-entering the civilian workforce.

Vocational rehabilitation had evolved from simple vocational guidance for physically disabled persons to a wide range of services whose purpose was to integrate disabled persons into the economic mainstream. In recognition of this change, under P.L. 113 the VR program was taken out of the Office of Education and became a separate office within the Federal Security Agency, the Office of Vocational Rehabilitation (OVR). Later, in 1953, OVR was made part of the new Department of Health, Education, and Welfare.

The broadening of the role of vocational rehabilitation continued with the passage of Public Law 565, the Vocational Rehabilitation Amendments of 1954, based on proposals by Mary Switzer, who had been appointed director of OVR. It provided $30 million in grants to the states and additional funds for a variety of purposes, including training of medical and rehabilitation professionals, research and development in rehabilitative medicine and rehabilitative engineering, the development of in-service training programs for rehabilitation workers, and the alteration of various facilities into rehabilitation centers and sheltered workshops. The 1954 amendments also permitted states to create separate departments of vocational rehabilitation outside of state educating agencies.

The development of vocational rehabilitation was

shaped by changing definitions in the role of the federal government brought about by the two world wars and the depression of the 1930s. A similar change took place with the next great expansion of federal responsibilities and activities, the Great Society programs of Lyndon Johnson's administration during the mid-1960s. The Vocational Rehabilitation Amendments of 1965 provided more federal funds, added to the array of VR services, and extended coverage to new client groups. Funding to the states was increased to $300 million, and the required state "match" was decreased from fifty-fifty to 75 percent federal and 25 percent state funding. The amendments included additional appropriations for innovative programs for research and development, for technical assistance to the states, and for building and staffing facilities such as sheltered workshops. Eligibility for VR services was extended to individuals with "socially handicapping conditions" as determined by a psychologist or psychiatrist, including adult criminal offenders and juvenile delinquents.

In 1968, expansion was carried still further. The federal-state proportions for financial support of state programs were changed to 80 percent federal and 20 percent state funds. Services were authorized to families of disabled persons and to clients after they became employed. Further, the Vocational Rehabilitation Amendments of 1968 authorized payment by the federal government of 90 percent of costs associated with vocational evaluations of "disadvantaged" persons, including poor people, ex-offenders, and other social pariahs.

The vocational rehabilitation program was employed by officials of the Johnson administration as an integral tool of its War on Poverty. Following a reorganization of HEW in 1967, OVR was made part of a Social and Rehabilitative Services Administration (SRS) within the department. SRS was headed by the former director of OVR, Mary Switzer, and also included the Children's

Bureau, the Administration on Aging, the Public Welfare Assistance Payments Administration, and the Medical Services Administration (responsible for Medicaid).

The concept of rehabilitation was at the core of the ideology of the emerging American welfare state. It was felt by reformers that individuals who could not function as full members of society because of physical or mental limitations, inadequate socialization, or blocked opportunities could participate more fully with training, counseling, and appropriate role models. However, the idea of individual rehabilitation was to be seen in subsequent years as inadequate. Rehabilitation would enable a disabled individual to participate in social institutions only to the extent that the individual's participation was welcome and not dependent on disruptive accommodations. The issue of barriers to access by disabled individuals was to attain overriding significance in the 1970s, with the growth of a civil rights movement within the disabled community. To understand the context within which that movement came about, however, it is important to understand the preceding models of earlier civil rights movements. Similarly, to understand the context for the enactment of Section 504, it is important to understand the preceding models of earlier civil rights legislation.

Civil Rights Models

The social movement that defined the concept of civil rights in the United States since World War II has been the movement for equality for black Americans. From the bus boycott in Montgomery in 1955 to the sit-ins in southern lunch counters by freedom riders in the early sixties to the 1963 march on Washington, the goals and strategies of black (and white) activists have been equated with the term civil rights and been adopted by others seeking social change. The Legal Defense Fund of the National Association for the Advancement of Colored People has served as a model for the strategic use of the court system to claim the right of participation, just as the civil disobedience tactics of groups such as the Southern Christian Leadership Conference and the Student Non-Violent Coordinating Committee have been emulated by a series of activist movements.

Similarly, the laws that have defined the terms of how American government would establish and protect the rights of subordinate groups were those passed to protect and benefit black Americans. The Civil Rights Act of 1964, which guaranteed access to employment, education, and public accommodations; the Voting Rights Act of 1965, which guaranteed access to political participation; and the Civil Rights Act of 1968, which guaranteed access to housing—all of these and others were passed specifically to end discrimination against black Americans, while establishing the powers and limits of government intervention for civil rights issues.

The law that was the specific model for Section 504 was the sixth part, or title, of the Civil Rights Act of 1964, generally referred to as Title VI. Title VI and the rest of the 1964 Civil Rights Act were passed following a year of extraordinary events. In 1963, demonstrators, led by Martin Luther King, Jr., staged nonviolent civil disobedience protests in Birmingham, Alabama, seeking to desegregate local facilities. More than 2,500 people were arrested, and many of the demonstrators were brutally treated by state and local authorities. After these events were vividly portrayed in the national news media, including television, demonstrations spread to at least seventy-five other southern cities. The protests culminated in a massive march on Washington, D.C., at which King delivered his historic "I Have A Dream" speech.

The substance of the Civil Rights Act of 1964 was pro-

posed by President John Kennedy in the summer of
1963.[6] Introduced by Hubert Humphrey in the Senate
and Emanuel Celler in the House, the legislation had
broad support but was opposed by a number of conservative Republicans and southern Democrats in key leadership positions. After President Kennedy's assassina-
tion, however, passage of the bill took on the almost
religious significance of fulfilling Kennedy's civil rights
26   mission. With pressure from President Johnson and
skillful negotiations by Senator Humphrey and Senate
Minority Leader Everett Dirksen, a Senate filibuster by
opponents lasting more than 534 hours was finally overcome and the Civil Rights Act of 1964 was enacted. The
act prohibited discrimination in public accommodations
(Title II), in employment (Title VII), and in programs receiving federal funds (Title VI).

The substance of Title VI was that any recipient of
federal funds was prohibited from discriminating on the
basis of race, color, or national origin: "No person in the
United States shall, on the grounds of race, color, or national origin, be excluded from participation in, be denied the benefits of, or be subjected to discrimination
under any program or activity receiving federal financial
assistance." The balance of Title VI called for the issuance of regulations by all federal departments and agencies, provided for judicial review of actions taken under
the title, exempted employment except where employment was the purpose of the federal assistance, and
exempted programs of insurance and guarantee. The
rationale behind Title VI was that, if the federal government was pursuing a policy of nondiscrimination, then
it should not allow anyone practicing discrimination to
benefit by receiving federal assistance. While the provision has been applied to a range of federally supported
programs, it has probably received the most attention
with regard to public school programs. Complementing

broader constitutional rights guaranteed via *Brown v. Board of Education* and subsequent judicial rulings,[7] Title VI mandates an active role on the part of the executive branch of the federal government in support of desegregation, by providing for the cutoff of federal funds to offending localities.[8]

To prohibit discrimination by those receiving public resources may appear reasonable. In practice, it has proved quite controversial. Nevertheless, in the late 1960s and early 1970s Title VI was an important tool used by the HEW Office for Civil Rights (OCR) in forcing the desegregation of public schools and state colleges and universities in the South.[9]

Beyond its direct effects, Title VI was to serve as an important model for legislation prohibiting discrimination against other subordinate groups. The first such application was on behalf of women. Title IX of the Education Amendments of 1972, enacted on July 1, 1972, was one of a number of laws protecting the rights of women by the 92nd Congress, including the Equal Rights Amendment and the Equal Employment Opportunity Act.[10] This provision prohibits discrimination on the basis of sex in all education programs receiving federal financial assistance in language taken directly from Title VI. Title IX, however, applies only to education programs, unlike the more general Title VI.[11]

Enforcement of Title IX, as with the education requirements under Title VI, became the responsibility of the HEW Office for Civil Rights. The development of regulations for the provision was lengthy and controversial, and Title IX requirements continue to be hotly debated. Title IX has been applied to curriculum, admissions, career counseling, and a number of other areas in education, but its most well-known and hotly disputed application has been the distribution of resources between men's and women's athletic programs.

Early Anti-Discrimination Laws Protecting Disabled People

Since Titles VI and IX were both important civil rights measures, when a means for protecting the rights of disabled people was sought, they became the models for governmental regulation of civil rights. These statutes were not the only legal precedents for Section 504, however. In the last sixty-five years, a number of public programs have been established for the benefit of disabled people, including vocational rehabilitation, social security, services for disabled veterans, and special education programs in the schools. Most of them took as their rationales both a societal obligation to provide for dependent disabled people and the assumption that there would be benefits to society from making disabled individuals economically and socially self-sufficient. While many of these programs had the avowed goal of promoting the integration of disabled people into society, they often served to isolate them through the creation of "special" or protected settings in special education classes, in sheltered workshops, and in hospitals and residential institutions.

Building up the skills of disabled people is only a partial answer to the problem of their isolation. In addition to their impairments, disabled people may be constrained by what others permit them to do and where others permit them to be. These constraints may be the product of discomfort or of sincere concern on the part of able-bodied gatekeepers. Whatever the motivation, the life chances for disabled people become limited by much more than their actual disabilities.

Disability advocates have claimed that legal protections were necessary to ensure that access not be denied prejudicially. Perhaps the first attempts to ensure greater access for disabled people through statutory protections were the guide dog laws and white cane laws. These laws were first enacted by a few states in the 1930s and by many other states in the 1950s and early 1960s. By 1966, some form of these laws had been passed in virtually every state in the nation. Guide dog laws permit access by blind individuals to public life by striking down restrictions on the use of guide dogs in public places and buildings, on common carriers, and in places of public accommodation that may not otherwise allow the presence of dogs. White cane laws facilitate use of public streets and buildings by blind people using white canes by prohibiting interference with such use and by requiring drivers of motor vehicles to take precautions upon seeing the use of a white cane.

It is not surprising that blind people, whose disability allows a relatively high degree of participation in the mainstream of everyday life, were particularly active in claiming full social participation as their due. Acting through organizations such as the National Federation of the Blind (NFB), they lobbied state legislatures to pass white cane and guide dog laws. They were assisted in this lobbying by the Lions Clubs International, a network of local men's service clubs whose major activities have included work on behalf of blind people.

White cane and guide dog laws set important legal precedents about the right of access to public places. However, in most cases their benefits were limited to blind persons and did not affect individuals with other disabilities.[12] Furthermore, many blind people do not use white canes or guide dogs and were not provided greater access by these statutes. Thus, while breaking important legal ground, the laws had limited impact.

One of the first civil rights–oriented measures affecting all disabled people was the Architectural Barriers Act of 1968, which as a federal law was national in scope. This act required that all new federal construction be made accessible to handicapped persons. Accessibility was defined in terms of what are called the ANSI standards, which were developed by the American National Standards Institute (ANSI) in 1961 as the result of a conference sponsored by the President's Committee on Employment of the Handicapped (PCEH) and the National Easter Seal Society for Crippled Children and Adults. The ANSI standards, which were updated in the 1970s, provide for a barrier-free design that permits physically disabled people access to bathrooms and drinking fountains and provides specifications for doorways, ramps, and elevators to make all or most of a facility accessible to wheelchair-bound persons and others with physical disabilities.

30

Support for legislation requiring barrier-free design in federal buildings became significant in the mid-1960s. Rehabilitation professionals within the federal government, acting on the advice of those working in public and private vocational rehabilitation agencies around the country, proposed that a commission be formed to study the problem of architectural barriers and make recommendations. Kay Arneson, the commission's first director, described its creation:

> As early as 1965 . . . we said it isn't only the disability of the individual and what the rehab delivery system provides to him that counts, it is what is happening in the environment that affects his capacity to live and work independently; and there had been some preliminary work done by essential voluntary agencies like Easter Seal and some of our state VR agencies and a few of the forward-looking state employment agencies, they said, "One of the biggest problems is that once you get these people trained, you can't get them into buildings, you can't get them into work, you can't get them to church, you can't get them to shop. So we'd better work on the environment.
>
> In 1965 we proposed and the Congress gave us authority for a National Commission on Architectural Barriers to the Rehabilitation of Handicapped People. . . . We had a three-year mandate and in two years we came up with a proposed law which was the first architectural barriers law.[13]

The commission issued its report in December 1967, and in the following year Congress passed the proposed law. However, there were no provisions in the 1968 law for enforcement, and the pattern of compliance by federal agencies was inconsistent at best.[14] Further, the law only applied to new facilities owned or leased by the federal government. This limited and essentially voluntary measure was only a small step toward guaranteeing access for disabled people. It did, however, help to legitimize the concept that the federal government should guarantee access to public services to disabled people.

31

A Social Movement of Disabled People

Most of the programs described here were conceived, established, and operated by able-bodied individuals. However, the most forceful and committed advocates for disability rights have often been disabled people themselves, who often had to claim participation on the basis of rights rather than of the good will and charity of philanthropists, the government, or the general public. In recent decades, increasing numbers of advocacy groups have been organized by disabled persons.

The development of such groups may be more problematic for disabled people than for other excluded groups. Many other groups have their own subcultures based on collective history, geography, or social class. Disabled people are spread across the various social classes and status groups in society and, if their disability is not severe, may spend nearly all of their time in the company of able-bodied persons. Disability is an individual experience in most cases, and a community of disabled people may not exist unless it is consciously built.

Of course there are exceptions. Individuals with disabilities stemming from a single cause may already share a great deal, particularly if they already share occupational or other ties as in the case of disabled war veterans or miners with black lung disease. Further, shared subcultures commonly develop among residents of particular institutions.[15] Nevertheless, Goffman has described the stigmatized as constituting categories rather than social groups.[16] While they do have a sense of sharing common characteristics, they may not have "a stable and embracing pattern of social interaction." However, members of such a category may develop many group-like tendencies:

32

> What one does find is that the members of a particular stigma category will have a tendency to come together into small social groups whose members all derive from the same category, these groups themselves being subject to overarching organization to varying degrees. And one also finds that when one member of the category happens to come in contact with another, both may be disposed to modify their treatment of each other by virtue of believing that they each belong to the same "group." Further, in being a member of the category, an individual may have an increased probability of coming into contact with any other member, and even forming a relationship with him as a result. A category, then, can function to dispose its members to group-formation and relationships, but its total membership does not thereby constitute a group.[17]

Goffman goes on to suggest that the stigmatized may seek representation by individuals or organizations who can communicate with the government, the press, and the general public. Such representatives may crusade for the use of less derogatory descriptive terms for themselves, speak to groups of the stigmatized and the normal, provide role models of social adjustment, and help the stigmatized share feelings and identity through publications. Until recently, organizations of those "representing" disabled people were more prevalent than organizations of disabled people themselves. Many groups were dominated by able-bodied civic leaders or by service providers, and such organizations frequently operated on the basis of stereotypes of dependency for the disabled people they sought to represent.

Despite the difficulties of building organizations led by disabled individuals, however, there has been a history of associations of disabled people. One of the earliest, founded in 1920 by World War I veterans, was the Disabled American Veterans (DAV). The DAV was chartered by Congress in 1932 and calls itself the "official voice of the disabled veteran." Organized as a nonprofit organization, the DAV currently has 700,000 members, one-quarter of whom are Vietnam era veterans. While the DAV has a legislative agenda and a Washington office, its major activity is counseling and serving as an advocate for individual veterans through a network of three hundred national service officers. These service officers provide assistance in filing claims for disability benefits, rehabilitation programs, and other services available to disabled veterans. The DAV has not been a major participant in promoting more general programs for disabled people, focusing essentially on the needs of disabled veterans.

Other early organizations were founded among specific disability groups, particularly blind people. In 1921, the American Association for Workers for the Blind and the American Association of Instructors of the Blind merged to form the American Foundation for the Blind (AFB). Led by Robert Irwin, the AFB campaigned for state financial assistance for blind persons, the development of educational opportunities, and the establishment of a one-fare privilege for interstate transportation that allowed blind persons to pay a single fare for themselves and a guide.[18] Another group was the National Federation of the Blind, perhaps the first organization of disabled people with a strong civil rights orientation. Founded in 1940, the NFB has been an often militant supporter of equal rights for blind and other disabled persons. Under the leadership of one of its founders, Jacobus tenBroek, a blind attorney who served as its president for over twenty years, the NFB was an important proponent of the guide dog and white cane laws.

Other organizations of disabled persons were established in the twenty years after World War II, including the Paralyzed Veterans of America (PVA), the National Association of the Deaf (NAD), the American Council of the Blind (ACB), the National Association for Retarded Citizens (NARC), and the United Cerebral Palsy Association. These organizations had varying degrees of political involvement, but none was oriented toward the general issue of civil rights for all disabled people. For the most part, each sought to advance the position of its specific constituency group. The organization with the most political involvement in advocacy for disabled people until the early 1970s was the National Rehabilitation Association (NRA), which represented professionals in the vocational rehabilitation field and did not include disabled recipients of services in its membership.

This pattern of representation by providers of services and by organizations with essentially parochial concerns was to change in the late 1960s. At that time changes were taking place within the community of those who identified themselves as disabled. Medical technology was extending the lives of those with a variety of medical problems or injuries who would previously not have survived, and the number of active disabled adults increased. Furthermore, medical and rehabilitative advances were giving those who in earlier times would have been totally incapacitated the potential to function in society, such as many who had survived the final polio epidemics of the 1950s.[19] For growing numbers of disabled people, physical impairment was becoming less handicapping than the barriers of stereotyping attitudes and architectural constraints.

Another development was the increase in the number of people experiencing disabling injuries in childhood, adolescence, and young adulthood. Most polio victims had clear memories of what it had been like to be able-bodied, as did teenagers who suffered paralyzing spinal cord injuries in automobile accidents and veterans of the Vietnam war who returned home with service-connected disabilities. Many of these people, who reached adulthood in the 1960s, had not incorporated a self-image of dependency to the same extent as those with congenital physical conditions. Their self-images and their expectations for themselves were radically different from those who had always thought of themselves as handicapped. They wanted to be able to function as normal young adults, both socially and economically. As a result of technological innovations, such participation was more often possible and, because of other social changes taking place, became a political objective as well as a personal goal.

In the communities and college campuses of this period were models of other groups seeking greater participation in social institutions and more autonomy and control in their lives. Demands for greater participation by disabled people occurred in the wake of the widespread and highly visible social conflicts of the 1960s. These conflicts included the struggle for civil rights by black people, the anti-war and student movements, and a revitalized feminist movement. A number of disabled people had been active participants in these movements, and they came to see their disability in the same political sense as blacks viewed their race or women their gender. Along with this new consciousness came an appreciation of how the change strategies of other movements could be adopted. While models of change-oriented advocacy did not guarantee success, they did suggest a method for stirring up latent support among a constituency and among the general public, and for channeling that support in attempts to influence governmental and institutional decision-makers.

The potential of integration into the societal mainstream was motivating disabled people to form new organizations at the local and state levels and to revitalize existing organizations. Groups took more militant stances, and many were willing to engage in demonstrations and civil disobedience. A number of the newly formed organizations included individuals with a variety of disabilities. One such organization was the Center for Independent Living (CIL) in Berkeley, California, which was founded by Ed Roberts, a quadriplegic who had virtually forced an unwilling University of California to admit him as a student in 1962.[20] CIL provided a variety of services to disabled individuals aimed at promoting their independence and included among its activities a major advocacy focus. Another group, Disabled in Action (DIA), was organized in New York City in 1971, founded by Judy Heumann, a wheelchair-bound teacher who had to bring suit against the City of New York in order to obtain her teaching certificate. By the spring of 1972, DIA had chapters in several other cities and 1,500 members.[21] Other local organizations founded in this period included the California Association of the Physically Handicapped and a group in Florida that called itself WARPATH (World Association to Remove Prejudice Against the Handicapped). These groups used tactics ranging from lawsuits to lobbying to demonstrations, adopting slogans such as "You've Given Us Your Dimes, Now Give Us Our Rights!"

A related development was the establishment of "public interest" legal centers that served as resources for disabled people on civil rights issues.[22] Staffed by legal activists, many of whom were not themselves disabled, these centers provided technical assistance to disability rights advocates. One of the first such centers was the National Center for Law and the Handicapped (NCLH), in South Bend, Indiana, which was sponsored by the University of Notre Dame School of Law, the American Bar Association, and the National Association for Retarded Citizens and received financial support from the Department of Health, Education, and Welfare. Other legal advocacy centers included the Public Interest Law Center of Philadelphia (PILCOP); the Children's Defense Fund (CDF), which has acted on behalf of disabled children; and the Institute for Public Interest Representation (INSPIRE), based at Georgetown University. All of these organizations were to become heavily involved in the political struggles over the implementation of Section 504.

In addition to grass-roots advocacy and legislative activity, the federal courts became an arena for efforts to establish the rights of disabled people. In the early 1970s, rulings in cases related to the treatment of disabled people by public institutions accorded disabled people many of the same constitutional rights to due process and equal protection as able-bodied people have. One of the earliest, *Wyatt v. Hardin*, established a "right to treatment" limiting indiscriminate institutionalization of mentally disabled persons.[23] Judge Frank Johnson ruled in 1971 that patients involuntarily committed to an Alabama mental hospital were being denied their constitutional rights to "receive such individual treatment as [would] give each of them a realistic opportunity to be cured or to improve his or her mental condition."

A second 1971 landmark case dealt with the related right to education of retarded children. In the case of *Pennsylvania Association for Retarded Children v. Commonwealth of Pennsylvania (PARC)*, the court held that the state owed retarded children an "appropriate" program of education and training.[24] After commenting on the efficacy of education and training for retarded children, who were frequently given essentially custodial care, the court ruled:

> It is the Commonwealth's obligation to place each mentally retarded child in a free, public program of education and training appropriate to the child's capacity, within the context of a presumption that, among the alternative programs of education and training required by statute to be available, placement in a regular public school class is preferable to placement in any other type of program of education and training.

38

The court ruling was made on the basis of both the Fourteenth Amendment (the equal protection clause of the Constitution) and expert testimony that any retarded child can benefit from education and training. The court concluded that education cannot be denied to retarded children while it is being provided to all other children through the public schools. The case was an important precursor to the Education for All Handicapped Children Act as well as to Section 504.

The following year in the District of Columbia, a similar guarantee to education was extended not just to mentally retarded but to all disabled children. The case, *Mills v. Board of Education* (*Mills*), involved claims by the plaintiffs that the District of Columbia was denying physically and mentally handicapped children due process by excluding them from publicly supported education and training.[25] The named plaintiff, Peter Mills, a black twelve-year-old in the fourth grade, had been excluded from school because he was alleged to be a behavior problem by his principal. The plaintiffs stated that, of approximately 22,000 children with disabilities in the District of Columbia, up to 18,000 were not being furnished with programs of specialized education.

The court ruling in *Mills* was similar to that in *PARC*. The district court held that the Board of Education was required to provide "whatever specialized education . . . will benefit" the excluded children and that excluding disabled children while providing education to able-bodied children was a violation of the due process protections of the Constitution. Another important element in the court ruling was that cost was not a justifiable reason for denying an education. The board of education had argued that providing such education would divert millions of dollars from other educational services. The court's reply was:

> If sufficient funds are not available to finance all of the services and programs that are needed and desirable in the system, then the available funds must be expended equitably in such a manner that no child is entirely excluded from a publicly supported education consistent with his needs and ability to benefit therefrom.

This principle had been followed in civil rights rulings before, when southern school districts claimed that they could not afford the cost of desegregating their schools. It was to appear again in the development of the regulations for Section 504.

Other cases highlighted additional practices that the courts judged to be discriminatory and unconstitutional treatment of disabled citizens. In an analysis of disability rights cases and Section 504, Martin H. Gerry and J. Martin Benton discern four distinct areas that directly applied constitutionally based rights to disabled people: the right to education, the right to treatment, the right to procedural fairness, and the right to equal participation.[26] They note that the courts provide the only clear thread of precedent leading up to the provision:

> Late 1973 appears in many ways an unlikely time for passage of Section 504. The first year of the second Nixon Administration was a time of rising anti–civil rights rhetoric. White House attention was focused on a variety of anti-busing proposals which had year by year gained strength both in number and in breadth of political support. Prior to

1973, very little attention had been given either by the Executive Branch or by Congress to the idea of civil rights for disabled people. Only in the courts had active conflicts arisen between those who insisted that disabled children and adults had a right to be free of discrimination and those who argued that the very notion of rights was likely to destroy the good will and charity which had allowed disabled people to advance as far as they had.[27]

40 By the early 1970s, several organizations were seeking to establish civil rights for disabled people through various strategies in a number of forums that included local, state, and federal legislative bodies, state and federal courts, the media, and the streets. None of these efforts, however, had opened doors for more than a handful of disabled individuals. The emerging struggle for disability rights was to be sustained through the decade of the seventies. One focus for these efforts was to be the United States Congress. However, some of the early civil rights victories for disability advocates were not of their own making. The enactment of a legislative guarantee of the right to access in federally supported programs, Section 504 of the Rehabilitation Act of 1973, came to be a central objective for the disability rights movement, but it was not itself a product of that movement.

The Genesis of Section 504

By 1972, concerns about permitting greater participation by disabled people in social institutions had been building among those involved with the developing organizations of disabled people and with the vocational rehabilitation program. These concerns were beginning to be voiced in terms borrowed from another social movement of the excluded—black Americans. In the 1960s, blacks had made emotionally powerful, and in many ways effective, demands for greater participation in white-dominated social institutions. While blacks did not gain full integration, many formal and traditional barriers to participation were struck down by statute and judicial ruling as a result. Civil rights evoked powerful symbols in American political ideology; the phrase had become linked with cultural and political values of equality, fair play, and opportunity.

The symbols and rhetoric of the black civil rights movement came to be used by those advocating the cause of greater access for disabled people as well. Disability rights advocates claimed that barriers to participation in the labor market and in government-supported services were often arbitrary, discriminatory, and not based on an accurate assessment of the capabilities of disabled people. Access for disabled people to societal institutions was sought as a basic civil right.

Characterizing access as a civil right had distinct political advantages. To portray access as another government benefit for disabled people, perhaps encouraged through the existing vocational rehabilitation network, would have defined improved access as desirable but not as a social imperative. Allowing disabled people greater participation thus would become an essentially charitable act. In periods of limited resources, which is to say virtually always, it is politically acceptable to limit benevolent acts of charity because of budgetary constraints, traditional practice, or administrative difficulty. Reducing benefits may be legitimate, while violating rights is not. Accordingly, many benefits have been claimed in recent years on the basis of rights—a right to health care, a right to education, a right to a job, a right to public assistance.

Rights are not established easily; the successful legitimation and institutionalization of rights typically results from political struggle. Bureaucratic decision-makers are unlikely to voluntarily acknowledge as rights what can become major claims on institutional resources. However, support for those claiming rights may be found from political officials concerned with coalition building or obtaining mass support. Elected officials, because of their need for the support of various constituencies, may be more willing to employ, or at least condone, a rhetoric of rights. Such rhetoric can be an effective symbolic way of communicating support for constituents' concerns. The short-term costs of supporting rights may be minimal, the political payoff may be substantial, and long-term effects are frequently discounted by officials looking to the next election.

The Civil Rights Act

By the early 1970s, the concept that disabled people had a civil right to broad social and economic participation was beginning to be accepted outside of the disability and rehabilitation community, and this acceptance was reflected in the United States Congress. In the 92nd Congress, legislation was introduced by two individuals with histories of support for both civil rights and health and human service systems, Senator Hubert Humphrey and Congressman Charles Vanik. On January 20, 1972, Senator Humphrey introduced on behalf of himself and Senator Charles Percy a bill to "amend the Civil Rights Act of 1964 in order to prohibit discrimination on the basis of physical or mental handicap in federally assisted programs."[1] The bill would have added "physical or mental handicap" to race, color, and national origin as illegal grounds for discrimination. Vanik's bill made the same addition.[2]

43

In introducing his bill, Humphrey proclaimed:

> The time has come when we can no longer tolerate the invisibility of the handicapped in America. . . . I am insisting that the civil rights of 40 million Americans now be affirmed and effectively guaranteed by Congress—our several million disabled war veterans, the 22 million people with a severe physically disabling condition, the one in every ten Americans who has a mental condition requiring psychiatric treatment, the six million persons who are mentally retarded, the hundreds of thousands crippled by accidents and the destructive forces of poverty, and the 100,000 babies born with defects each year.
>
> These people have the right to live, to work to the best of their ability—to know the dignity to which every human being is entitled. But too often we keep children, who we regard as "different" or a "disturbing influence," out of our schools and community activities altogether, rather than help them develop their abilities in special classes and programs. Millions of young persons and adults who want to learn a trade, work like other people, and establish their self-worth through a paycheck are barred from our vocational training programs and from countless jobs they could perform well. And yet we have sufficient statistics clearly demonstrating the benefits to the national economy and the investment return of income tax revenues resulting

from vocational rehabilitation and job placement for these citizens. Where is the cost-effectiveness in consigning them to public assistance or "terminal" care in an institution?

These are people who can and must be helped to help themselves. That this is their constitutional right is clearly affirmed in a number of recent decisions in various judicial jurisdictions. Every child—gifted, normal, and handicapped—has a fundamental right to educational opportunity and the right to health.[3]

Humphrey went on to cite estimates that only 40 percent of handicapped children were receiving needed special education and that entry to any public schooling was being denied to over one million children, including those with crippling conditions, mental retardation, and emotional disturbances.

The bills introduced by Humphrey and Vanik were similar to what would become Section 504 of the Rehabilitation Act. No hearings were held on the bills, however, and neither was brought to a vote in committee or on the floor of either house. That there is no record of attempts to secure passage for either bill is not unusual; introducing legislation is frequently only a signal of a legislator's position on an issue. Further, there may have been good reasons not to advance the proposals. Any expansion of Civil Rights Act coverage was controversial. Although there is no record of what happened when the bills were referred to the House and Senate Judiciary Committees, it may be that they were killed by committee liberals. The bills do not appear to have been opposed by conservatives blocking change for ideological reasons, nor by those responding to protests from the recipients of federal funds who would have been required to comply with the proposed amendments. Rather, the opposition apparently came from those who were committed to protecting the groups already covered by Title VI of the Civil Rights Act, notably blacks.

In earlier Congresses, southern Democrats and other conservatives had attempted to weaken existing civil rights legislation by expanding coverage beyond the capacity for enforcement, and civil rights advocates were concerned that any significant broadening of the scope of the Civil Rights Act would necessarily distract from and thus diminish enforcement of the existing provisions. Whatever the motivation, the amendments were not seriously considered.

45

Rehabilitation Act

The next attempt at providing protection for the civil rights of disabled people took place within another Senate committee, the Committee on Labor and Public Welfare, in its consideration of the Rehabilitation Act.[4] Although that committee had little previous involvement with civil rights, it did have a history of responsiveness to the concerns of labor and the impoverished. One of the most liberal and activist committees in Congress at the time, the Labor and Public Welfare Committee had been a center of support for a number of the more progressive statutes of the Nixon-Ford years, including the Education for All Handicapped Children Act, the Occupational Safety and Health Act, and the Child Development Act.

One of the tasks before this liberal body in 1972 was the renewal of the vocational rehabilitation program, which was also the responsibility of the Committee on Education and Labor in the House of Representatives. Following congressional procedure, both committees held hearings and prepared versions of bills reauthorizing the VR program and amending the existing statute. Most of this work was carrried out by the House committee, under the leadership of Congressman John Brademas. The House bill was based on the recommendations of the group representing rehabilitation professionals, the National Rehabilitation Association, and its legislative director, E. B. Whitten. Several provisions in the bill, however, did come from the Senate Subcommittee on the Handicapped, a part of the Labor and Public Welfare Committee. The subcommittee was chaired by Senator Jennings Randolph; other members included Harrison Williams, Alan Cranston, Jacob Javits, and Robert Stafford. All of the members were moderately liberal, and had staff doing their committee work who shared their political perspective.

Senator Randolph asked Senator Cranston, the ranking majority member, to take responsibility for developing the Rehabilitation Amendments of 1972; Cranston chaired the hearings on the legislation and managed the bill on the Senate floor.

The procedure adopted for reauthorization of the Rehabilitation Act is typical of the way most legislation is handled by Congress. After a bill is introduced, it is referred to a committee, which holds hearings to gather information and expert opinion. Following the hearings the bill is redrafted, or "marked up," with changes typically negotiated by staff members representing the subcommittee or committee members. (The staff people involved with the rehabilitation bill, and their patrons, are listed in Figure 1.)

The general attitude of congressional committee members and staff toward legislation in 1972 reflected the political context of the time. The early 1970s was a period of serious institutional conflict between Congress and the president. Issues of contention included presidential "impoundment" or withholding of funds appropriated by Congress, the manner in which mandated programs were being administered by often hostile executive agencies, and disagreements over disengagement from the Vietnam war. Many of those working on

Figure 1: Major Congressional Staff Involved with
Section 504 in 1972–73

Member of Congress	Staff Member
Senate	
Alan Cranston (D.–Calif.)	Michael Burns
	Jonathan Steinberg
Harrison Williams (D.–N.J.)	Nik Edes
	Lisa Walker
Jennings Randolph (D.–W. Va.)	Patria Forsythe
	Robert Humphreys
Robert Stafford (R.–Vt.)	Michael Francis
Jacob Javits (R.–N.Y.)	Roy Millenson
House of Representatives	
John Brademas (D.–Ind.)	Jack Duncan
Albert Quie (R.–Minn.)	Martin LaVor

Capitol Hill, particularly younger staff with a liberal activist perspective, viewed the role of Congress as involving the enactment of sweeping reforms that would elicit some kind of response from President Nixon and his administration, but the means by which such reforms were to be implemented and administered was not an overriding concern. In fact, if a recalcitrant executive branch had problems in administering a program, so much the better. Congressional critics could charge that the administration was inept, illiberal, and willing to subvert laws passed by Congress.

Thus Congress was willing and often eager to throw down a liberal gauntlet. Nik Edes, who was on Senator Williams's staff, describes this attitude:

> You have to understand that the 1970s began really the emergence of the Congress as an institution in really initiat-

ing substantial amounts of social policy, important social policy. We had an executive which at the time was considered to be the enemy, for a lot of reasons. We in the Congress therefore as a matter of self defense and as a matter of Democratic Party politics felt that it was important to take the initiative because otherwise the initiative would not be taken elsewhere.[5]

48 It was a time for sweeping gestures, attempts to help people, with social and economic costs considered not as important as potential benefits and the political opportunities that might be gained. Edes continued:

I'll tell you the frame of mind we all had. We had lived for three years under Richard Nixon, and under being told no, no, no, no, no by an executive branch which was totally unresponsive to the programs of the sixties, and to the things that were still felt important during that time of the seventies by a vast majority of the Congress. . . . We were angry at the Nixon administration, and we wanted to do everything we could to do as much as we could to help people. Whether it be disabled people, minorities, poor people, you name it. Even the middle class. . . .

It was an important thread running through everything that was done at those times. It was: I'll get those sons of bitches, they don't want to show any positive inclination toward doing things at all, then we're going to really stick it to them. And in the process, help people. I mean I don't think that those are necessarily incompatible goals.

Another Senate staff member, Robert Humphreys, who was counsel to the full Labor and Public Welfare Committee, described a similar climate of liberal opposition:

You have to recall the milieu in which the revised Rehabilitation Act was developed. The Labor Committee at that time was a highly liberal, activist committee, and they were in the middle of reacting, I suppose, to Richard Nixon. And there were a lot of service programs frequently in defiance of the then Administration.

It was within this context that Congress considered the Rehabilitation Act of 1972. The vocational rehabilitation program was due for reauthorization, and its revised version contained a number of proposals for new programs. Many of these proposals were developed in response to an evaluation of the VR program conducted by Congress's auditing and investigative unit, the General Accounting Office (GAO).[6]

The Rehabilitation Act of 1972 was designed to expand and improve the vocational rehabilitation program. In addition to this change in emphasis, the bill had a number of other provisions. It authorized additional funding to existing VR programs and created several programs for serving disability groups with special problems. The eligibility definition was also changed to bring more severely disabled individuals into the VR program. There was a shift from an almost exclusive emphasis on preparing clients for work to a more general rehabilitation program that would promote independent living for those not capable of regular or perhaps any employment. In accordance with this change in emphasis, the word "vocational" was dropped from the title of the bill. In the interests of advocacy and policy coordination, an Office of the Handicapped was created within HEW. To implement the 1968 Architectural Barriers Act, an Architectural Barriers Compliance Board was established as well.

As it was initially drafted, the legislation did not include Section 504. Nor was Section 504 suggested at any of the hearings held on the proposed law. Rather, the section was conceived by Senate committee staff members and added to the bill at a relatively late point in the legislative process. That the proposal for Section 504 came from staff rather than from members of Congress themselves was not unusual. Although congressmen and senators set overall policy directions, the demands on their time mean that most of them delegate the details of legislating and constitutent service to their staffs.

Senior staff often make a number of day-to-day decisions that are later ratified by their bosses, whose wide range of responsibilities require reliance on staff expertise.[7] The development of the Rehabilitation Act was typical of this expanded staff role. Members of the involved committees in the House and Senate were kept informed on the progress of the evolving bill, but most of the actual development and revision of the act was conducted by committee staffs. This was the case for the inclusion of Section 504.

Among staff members for the House Education and Labor Committee, Jack Duncan had been an assistant to the long-time commissioner of rehabilitation, Mary Switzer, and had close ties to the rehabilitation community. Such rehabilitation experience was lacking among the Senate staff involved with the Rehabilitation Act, but they were interested in helping disabled people. One Senate staff member, Robert Humphreys, recalled "a willingness and interest and a desire to do good for disabled people. There were a lot of advocates." The Senate staff had more experience with civil rights issues. Lisa Walker described the staff as including a number of people who were marginally familiar with Title VI and Title VII (which covers employment) of the Civil Rights Act and labor lawyers such as Nik Edes, who had been involved with affirmative action issues. Jon Steinberg had experience with health issues, though not with disability. Michael Francis had no involvement in either. Walker was a political scientist by training who had been an intern working for John Brademas and later for Harrison Williams. Walker, perhaps the figure on the Senate committee staff involved with Section 504 most centrally in later years, had had very limited experience with disability issues while working for Jack Duncan on Brademas's staff. When Senator Williams became chair of the full Labor and Public Welfare Committee in 1970 and was searching for issues that he could stake out for himself and the committee, he picked up disability as an area in which no one in the Senate was working in a concentrated way. Walker remembered that it seemed "an obvious direction to take" for Williams and thus for her.

The summer of 1972 was a time when civil rights was an issue with high visibility in Congress. Creation of a single civil rights agency within the federal government to oversee and coordinate enforcement of the various civil rights statutes was being debated at the time, as was the desegregation of the construction trades through the recently developed Philadelphia Plan. Senator Cranston had recently examined the Labor Department's monitoring of affirmative action by federal contractors and was concerned about the politicization of civil rights enforcement. These experiences may have influenced Cranston's staff and other committee staff against centralized civil rights programs and toward the decentralized approach employed in Section 504.

51

The Drafting of Section 504

The idea for including an anti-discrimination prohibition in the Rehabilitation Act occurred toward the end of a meeting held in late August to discuss revision of the marked-up rehabilitation bill. Participants in the meeting included Jon Steinberg, Michael Francis, Nik Edes, Lisa Walker, Michael Burns, Roy Millenson, and Robert Humphreys. Staff members were concerned that, when disabled individuals completed their training in the VR system and were ready to enter the workplace, many employers appeared to be reluctant to hire them. Staff members felt that the final goal of the VR program, getting disabled people into the mainstream of society, was being blocked by negative attitudes and discrimination on the part of employers and others.

Someone suggested that language be included in the

Rehabilitation Act proscribing discrimination against handicapped people in federally assisted programs. Such a provision would be comparable to the provisions of Title VI of the Civil Rights Act of 1964, and to Title IX of the Education Amendments of 1972, but would not involve amending those statutes. Roy Millenson of Senator Javits's staff had been involved in the development of the Education Amendments, and he ran out to his office and brought back language from Title VI. The language was adapted and inserted at the very end of the Rehabilitation Act. In the version of the bill that was ultimately enacted, that provision became Section 504.

The last title of the Rehabilitation Act included three other civil rights provisions protecting disabled people. Two dealt with employment and architectural accessibility within the federal government, while the third concerned employment by federal contractors.[8] Each of those provisions was a potentially important guarantee of access, yet none had the broad potential impact of the final civil rights section, which was to apply to any activity or program receiving federal support.

Section 504 was a single sentence at the very end of the Rehabilitation Act that read: "No otherwise qualified handicapped individual in the United States, as defined in Section 7(6), shall, solely by reason of his handicap, be excluded from the participation in, be denied the benefits of, or be subjected to discrimination under any program or activity receiving Federal financial assistance." At the time of its inclusion and throughout the consideration of the Rehabilitation Act by Congress and the president, neither members of Congress nor those concerned with disability issues took note of the section. This would change. Within a few years, Section 504 would be seen as landmark legislation, bearing both tremendous costs and benefits. One leading disability rights activist was to write:

It is Section 504 that contains the greatest promise. . . . Virtually every area of modern American life is inexorably intertwined with federal financial assistance and this is why the protection Section 504 offers is so important. It offers the one unifying key to mainstreaming of the disabled population into the general community on all fronts in a cohesive and orderly manner. . . .

Section 504 is historic in its scope and depth, the single most important civil rights provision ever enacted on behalf of disabled citizens in this country.[9]

53

It might be thought that such a far-reaching measure would have involved substantial debate on its merits, and that Congress would carefully indicate its intentions when considering the legislation. However, there is little in the record to suggest what, if anything, members of Congress had in mind when Section 504 was enacted. When a bill is considered in Congress, both the committees that prepare it and the conference committee that reconciles the House and Senate versions issue reports. These reports provide the opportunity to comment on the statutory language and provide background information referred to as "legislative history." The legislative history of the Rehabilitation Act contains only passing references to Section 504, stating simply that the section prohibits discrimination, without providing any rationale or predicting any impact. The committee reports may also contain projections on the cost for each of the statutory provisions. Unlike most of the other parts of the Rehabilitation Act, no public expenditures were projected for Section 504. Legislative history also consists of the discussion of a bill during its consideration on the House and Senate floors, which is published in the *Congressional Record*. No references were made to the potential significance of Section 504 on the floor of either house. In short, there was nothing to indicate what Congress had intended when it had passed Section 504.

It appears that most members of Congress either were unaware that Section 504 was included in the act or saw the section as little more than a platitude, a statement of a desired goal with little potential for causing institutional change. The initial consideration of the Rehabilitation Act proceeded smoothly, and the legislation was approved by committees and by each house of Congress. Apparently considered noncontroversial, at each vote taken the act was unanimously approved.

The bill, including Section 504, was transmitted to the White House for consideration. In a surprising rejection of Congress's bipartisan work, President Nixon refused to sign the bill, thereby killing it through a pocket veto. The President's veto message of October 27, 1972, justifies his action on the grounds of the Rehabilitation Act's costs, its creation of new programs and advisory structures, and its specificity, which he claimed would constrain the authority of the executive branch. No reference was made to the bill's civil rights provisions.

After the 1972 elections, one of the first orders of business for the new Congress was to reintroduce the Rehabilitation Act in essentially the same form and to hold hearings on the substitute bill.[10] Testimony at the hearings for the most part deplored the veto. There was only one comment on Section 504, by John Nagle, director of the National Federation of the Blind's Washington office. At the time, the NFB was one of the few groups representing disabled people that had a lobbying capacity, and it was also one of the most vocal national organizations favoring civil rights laws protecting disabled people. Nagle testified:

> The provision . . . prohibiting discrimination against the physically and mentally impaired in any Federally assisted program is of major consequence to all disabled people as they strive to surmount the difficulties and disadvantages of their disabilities and endeavor to attain a normal, pro-

ductive and fulfilling life. This civil rights for the handicapped provision . . . brings the disabled within the law when they have been so long outside of the law. It establishes that because a man is blind or deaf or without legs, he is not less a citizen, that his rights of citizenship are not revoked or diminished because he is disabled. But most important of all, the civil rights for the handicapped provision . . . creates a legal remedy when a disabled man is denied his rightful citizenship rights because of his disability. It gives him a legal basis for recourse to the courts that he may seek to remove needless barriers, unnecessary obstacles and unjustified barricades that impede or prevent him from functioning fully and in full equality with all others.[11]

55

After the hearings were completed, the House and the Senate once again passed the Rehabilitation Act (now of 1973) by overwhelming margins. Again, the president vetoed the bill. An attempt was made to override the veto, but it failed in the Senate by four votes, since a number of Republican senators felt obliged to support the president. Once again, Section 504 was not at issue in the veto.

The Rehabilitation Act was introduced for a third time, on May 23, 1973. Finally, Congress yielded to some of the president's concerns, cutting down on the amount of funds authorized, the number of new programs begun, and the autonomy of the Rehabilitative Services Administration (RSA) within HEW. In September of 1973, Congress passed the amended bill. While the amendments did not meet all of President Nixon's objections, he was willing to support it, and on September 26, 1973, the bill was signed into law as the Rehabilitation Act of 1973, Public Law 93-112.

The debate over the presidential vetoes of the earlier versions of the Rehabilitation Act was the occasion for some of the earliest demonstrations in Washington by disabled individuals. Following the first veto of the act, a demonstration was organized by people who were attending the annual conference of the President's Committee on Employment of the Handicapped. Since 1948, the PCEH has held yearly conferences in Washington to honor outstanding disabled individuals and employers of disabled persons and to provide a forum for the discussion of vocational rehabilitation issues. Although the PCEH was perceived by younger and more militant disabled people as conservative, the conferences were widely attended and provided the opportunity for disparate groups to get to know one another. Several of those attending developed a network that was notable for its crosscutting of disability categories. Previously, little contact had been established among blind, deaf, and orthopedically impaired persons. Disabled veterans formed separate veterans' groups, which focused on the Veterans Administration (VA). Individuals with epilepsy, cerebral palsy, and a wide range of other diseases and conditions formed their own organizations. Parents of disabled children did not work with adult disability groups. At the PCEH in the early seventies, however, there began to be more communication among these groups.

The development of coalitions was encouraged when individuals attending the PCEH conference in 1972 were outraged by President Nixon's veto. One person involved was Eunice Fiorito, a blind social worker from New York City, an organizer of a local cross-disability group called Disabled in Action, and the first director of the New York City Mayor's Office for the Handicapped. She described the first demonstration:

> In 1972 we planned a demonstration at the Lincoln Monument. We all came out of the President's Committee the night of the big banquet, all of the kids had this march and demonstration and then had this all-night vigil, over at the Lincoln Monument. I went to the banquet in my very for-

mal outfit and then [demonstrated] in the rain for about six hours.

The meetings of the PCEH came to serve as a focus for expressions of solidarity and advocacy for the disabled community. At the 1973 conference, another demonstration was held in support of the Rehabilitation Act, with 150 disabled demonstrators marching down Washington's Connecticut Avenue. But despite the demonstrations, disability advocates had not organized sufficiently to exert influence directly on the federal legislative process. In the early 1970s, lobbying was practiced only by the more established organizations, many of which were oriented toward service providers. Most of those groups were more interested in expanded benefits than in civil rights guarantees, with some notable exceptions, such as the National Federation of the Blind.

Section 504 was not developed at the urging of representatives of disabled people, although some have subsequently made this claim. All of those interviewed from the House and Senate committee staffs provide the same account of the genesis of Section 504—that it was an initiative of liberal congressional staff and not done at the request, suggestion, or demand of outside groups. Jonathan Steinberg, for example, described the section as having had no visible proponents before 1974. Robert Humphreys remembers Section 504 as "essentially a self-generated item on the part of staff of the [Labor and Public Welfare] committee." Nik Edes states that the Senate staff were "the Martin Luther Kings of the disability movements on Capitol Hill and in the government. . . . The movement [of disabled people] was stimulated by the acts of a very few individuals who were in the legislative branch."

Some critics of Section 504 have stated that its drafting and passage was essentially a fluke and that its impact was not anticipated.[12] But those who were responsible for writing the section deny that. While most agree that all the implications of the section were not known at the time, they also contend that, when they included Section 504 in the Rehabilitation Act, as Robert Humphreys said, "there was a feeling that it would have a profound effect." Lisa Walker characterized the broadness and simplicity of the section as typical of the times. She stated that many of those working on the Hill were not lawyers and had never litigated, and they did not see the need to legislate all policies in specific words. She cited programs of the 1960s that had been drafted very simply with a broad statement of congressional intent, with the confidence that the administration would carry them out. She stressed the fact that the nature of Section 504 was not unintended but was rather a different approach to writing legislation than the more explicit and detailed one used in the later 1970s.

While committee staff drafting Section 504 claim to have known what they were doing, members of Congress clearly were not generally aware that the Rehabilitation Act included a section modeled on Title VI of the Civil Rights Act that provided for civil rights guarantees that would affect every federal grantee. Taken as a general statement of purpose, Section 504 might be hard to argue with. As Jack Duncan, chief majority staff member in the House Labor and Education Committee, asked:

> What more reasonable position than to say that if people are to receive federal funds or assistance, they should not discriminate? How can anyone argue against that? And at the time they didn't, mainly because they didn't have a chance. Title V of the Rehabilitation Act was submerged with a lot of other legislation going through at the same time, which drew more attention.

Robert Humphreys gave essentially the same picture:

There was very little discussion of it, its substance or content, in either house or in committee, other than merely some discussions within the committee mark-up sessions that this was similar to the Civil Rights Act and that this would be protective of disabled people's rights in employment and would counter some of the discriminatory practices that had been pervasive throughout the country as far as disabled people were concerned.

After the Rehabilitation Act was signed, responsibility for Section 504 passed to the executive branch of the federal government. The Department of Health, Education, and Welfare was to be responsible for defining what this simple provision meant and how it was to be implemented.

4 Writing the Regulation for Section 504

Section 504 of the Rehabilitation Act of 1973 became law in September 1973. However, it was by no means clear how this statement of nondiscrimination was to be translated into government policy and put into effect. The provision was largely unknown outside of Congress, and not particularly well known within Congress. There was no guidance in the Rehabilitation Act or its legislative history on how or when discrimination on the basis of handicap was to be eliminated in federally assisted programs or on what constituted illegal discrimination. Conceivably, Section 504 could have remained a simple statement of good intentions.[1] However, the responsibility for the section's implementation was assigned to the HEW Office for Civil Rights, an agency whose staff was strongly committed to governmental activism and social change. As a result of this assignment and of the language of the provision with its strong civil rights precedents, Section 504 was to go beyond being an expression of support for disabled people to serve as the basis for a far-reaching regulatory agenda.

Assignment

Once the president had approved the Rehabilitation Act, the Department of Health, Education, and Welfare assumed authority for its implementation.[2] Unlike the rest of the Rehabilitation Act and most other federal legislation, Section 504 contained no provision for its own implementation. That is, Congress did not express its intentions as to which agency was to carry out the law, whether regulations were to be issued, and exactly who was to be subject to them.

In the absence of a legislative history, the HEW officials charged with planning for Section 504's implementation wrote a letter to the Senate Labor and Public Welfare Committee asking what to do. The senators who were members of the Subcommittee on the Handicapped responded to the newly appointed secretary of HEW, Caspar Weinberger,[3] that he had a statutory mandate to administer the Rehabilitation Act and therefore had the implicit authority to "see that all provisions of the Act are fully and effectively carried out." They described the secretary as "the most logical and qualified person within the Federal Government to oversee implementation of and to enforce [Section 504]." The senators also sought to maintain their involvement with Section 504 by encouraging cooperation between congressional staff and HEW staff in the development of regulations for the section.

Once it was established that Section 504 was HEW's responsibility, department officials had to delegate authority for the measure to one of HEW's component agencies. The logical choice for any disability legislation would have been the agency traditionally responsible for disability programs, the Rehabilitative Services Administration. RSA had the greatest expertise on disability issues within the department. At the time, RSA was part of the Social and Rehabilitative Services Administration, which also was responsible for welfare services and Medicaid, so responsibility for Section 504 was initially offered to SRS. However, due to objections raised by Jim Dwight, the administrator of SRS, another agency had to be selected.[4] The nature of those objections are not documented, but the enforcement of a civil rights statute would have been a significant departure from the traditional SRS welfare orientation and the RSA mission of operating the network of VR programs.

Assignment of Section 504 to the HEW Office of General Counsel (OGC) was also considered. OGC, which provides legal services to the department, had great expertise on regulatory and administrative law. However, OGC has traditionally avoided program administration, and the secretary decided not to break this tradition.

62

Neither RSA nor OGC had experience in administering a civil rights provision such as Section 504. The agency that seemed best suited for administration was the Office for Civil Rights, which was already responsible for two civil rights measures with language similar to Section 504—Title VI of the Civil Rights Act and Title IX of the Education Amendments of 1972. Weinberger's decision to assign Section 504 to OCR does not appear to have been based on a thorough consideration of the implications of the differences among OCR, RSA, and OGC. Rather, it was made routinely because of the language of the section, which had been somewhat impulsively adapted from Title VI. The decision was to have important consequences for the substance of the regulation.

This question of assignment was not a trivial question of bureaucratic politics. The shape of 504 would be the result of whoever interpreted it. The issue of civil rights for disabled people was to be approached in very different terms by the lawyers in the Office of Civil Rights and the rehabilitation professionals of the Rehabilitative Services Administration. Although both groups are committed to greater participation in society by disabled people, OCR staff members tend to stress legally established rights and procedures, whereas RSA staff members place greater emphasis on community education and voluntary compliance.

The view of strategies to increase access for disabled

people held by officials in the Rehabilitative Services Administration, many of whom were rehabilitation professionals, was that social participation is gradually achieved by building skills among disabled people and by educating the rest of society about their capabilities. Like many others in the "helping professions," they emphasized voluntary action and the development of consensus. If Section 504 had fallen within the responsibilities of the RSA, the traditional rehabilitation services agency, the regulation might have been far less stringent and far reaching.

Within OCR, the emphasis on formal rules and an adversarial relationship with regulated institutions was in part the product of the professional ideology of its staff attorneys.[5] OCR's institutional perspective was also influenced by its history. Since its founding in the mid-1960s, the office had been in the forefront of attempts by the federal government to break down the barriers of racial segregation. OCR's efforts were largely focused on desegregating public educational systems, often in the face of opposition by uncooperative or hostile public officials and community leaders.[6] OCR staff were thus generally unwilling to rely upon voluntary cooperation and the avowed good intentions of those whose discriminatory behavior they were trying to change. They sought formally established protections against discrimination and tended to view recipients of federal funds with suspicion.

The OCR staff's uncompromising approach has been explored in Jeremy Rabkin's study of the office, which focuses on how OCR's organizational mission has been defined.[7] According to Rabkin, civil rights are not considered fair game for the give and take of compromise generally characteristic of American politics, and within OCR questions of cost and agency effectiveness were considered less relevant than upholding strict standards of civil rights, which were felt to be legally and morally absolute. While OCR staff would approach problems informally and attempt to resolve complaints through negotiation and compromise, they believed that the federal government should assist people in claiming rights established by statute. Where negotiation was ineffective, they sought to establish administrative and legal mechanisms for the guarantee of rights. Furthermore, a variety of specific actions were required of federal fund recipients, even in the absence of actual complaints. The OCR staff did not consider factors affecting recipients such as cost, inconvenience, and disruption of existing programs to be legitimate reasons for failing to meet requirements of nondiscrimination.

64

Initiating the Rulemaking Process

The OCR director, Peter Holmes, assigned responsibility for Section 504's implementation to his newly appointed deputy, Martin Gerry, who was in charge of the development of OCR policy. Gerry had been involved in another OCR effort to deal with new questions of defining discrimination. He had written the office's memorandum for the landmark court case *Lau v. Nichols*, which dealt with the exclusion of non-English-speaking children from public education and the extent of special accommodation the District of Columbia public schools needed to make for such children.[8] *Lau* was to become important in defining public policy on bilingual education and set precedents on disregarding cost when acting to guarantee equal access to public facilities.

Gerry supervised regulation development and policymaking for Section 504, but assigned the day-to-day responsibility for the section to John Wodatch. A staff attorney with five years of OCR experience, Wodatch felt that the job provided him with a good opportunity to be in charge of a big project from start to finish and to gain experience with policy development. Neither Wodatch nor Gerry had been involved previously with the issue of discrimination on the basis of handicap.

Wodatch's first responsibility was to assemble a staff. The HEW Office of General Counsel assigned Ann Beckman, also an attorney, to the project. Ten additional temporary positions were authorized, with personnel to be drawn from other parts of OCR for temporary assignments. Only two of the new staff had experience with disability issues—Raymond (Bud) Keith, who was disabled, and Ed Lynch, an attorney who had worked on mental retardation issues in Massachusetts and for the President's Committee on Mental Retardation.

Next Wodatch had to decide how to approach implementation of the ambiguous statutory language by trying to find out what exactly Congress had in mind when it passed Section 504. OCR staff felt that the absence of a formal statement of intent could cast doubts on any decisions they made. If they needed to defend the rationale for the work, then informal discussions with Senate aides were not going to be sufficient. Meetings were held with staff from the Senate Labor and Public Welfare Committee, in particular with Harrison Williams's aides, Lisa Walker and Nik Edes.

One apparent problem was the program-specific definition of a handicapped individual in the Rehabilitation Act, which would have seriously limited the applicability of Section 504. The definition in the act was tied to the original purpose of the vocational rehabilitation program, the provision of employment. The definition in Section 7(6) of the 1973 act read:

> The term "handicapped individual" means any individual who (A) has a physical or mental disability which for such individual constitutes or results in a substantial handicap to employment and (B) can reasonably be expected to benefit in terms of employability from vocational rehabilitation services provided pursuant to Titles I and III of this Act.

65

This definition had been drafted for vocational training and counseling programs and did not cover a number of groups of people who might suffer from discrimination on the basis of handicap in federally supported programs. It excluded severely handicapped people and others who were not capable of being employed, including children and the elderly. Also excluded were individuals whose disabilities interfered with participation in nonemployment activities, such as public transportation. The definition also excluded those who were not disabled, but were subject to discrimination based on a past disability, such as a cardiac condition that had been successfully treated or a previous nervous breakdown, or a perceived disability, such as epilepsy, which is unlikely to interfere with employment or any other major life activity.

Both the inappropriate definition and the lack of legislative history were addressed by the Senate Subcommittee on the Handicapped in a post hoc manner following the meetings with OCR staff. In the summer of 1974, a series of "technical and clarifying" amendments for the Rehabilitation Act were proposed and enacted as the Rehabilitation Act Amendments of 1974. A new definition of handicapped individual was drafted by the OCR and Senate staffs, Section 111(a):

> For the purposes of Titles IV and V of this Act, such term (handicapped individual) means any person who (A) has a physical or mental impairment which substantially limits one or more of such person's major life activities, (B) has a record of such impairment, or (C) is regarded as having such an impairment.[9]

The conference committee that was responsible for reconciling the House and Senate versions of the Rehabilitation Act Amendments (the differences between these versions are not relevant to Section 504) issued a report to accompany the amendments as legislative history for them and, retroactively, for the 1973 act as well. One portion of this report provided a legislative history for Section 504 by discussing the parallels between Section 504, Title VI, and Title IX and the intent of Congress that steps be taken to implement the anti-discrimination section:

> Section 504 was patterned after, and is almost identical to, the anti-discrimination language of Section 601 of the Civil Rights Act of 1964 . . . and section 901 of the Education Amendments of 1972. . . . The section therefore constitutes the establishment of a broad government policy that programs receiving Federal financial assistance shall be operated without discrimination on the basis of handicap. It does not specifically require the issuance of regulations or expressly provide for enforcement procedures, but it is clearly mandatory in form, and such regulations and enforcement are intended.[10]

An oversight in the original drafting of Section 504 had made clarification of this enforcement intent necessary. Section 504 does not include provisions comparable to provisions in Title VI and Title IX, which explicitly call for regulations to be issued and provide remedies to people experiencing discrimination prohibited under those acts, establishing mechanisms by which the government and injured parties can seek to end discrimination. The OCR attorneys sought similar explicit authority for Section 504. The conference report established such authority and specifically delegated it to HEW because of the department's "experience in dealing with handicapped persons and with the elimination of discimination in other areas."[11] The report went on to describe the anticipated enforcement procedures, including investigation and review of federal aid recipients, informal negotiations, and formal sanctions, including cutting off funding. The report was issued on November 26, 1974, and optimistically expressed the conference committee's expectation that Section 504 regulations would be completed by the close of 1974.

Drafting a Regulation

The Rehabilitation Act Amendments of 1974 passed Congress and became law on December 7, 1974, and the Office for Civil Rights staff was able to proceed with a more substantial legislative mandate. They next sought to identify major issues to be resolved in the regulation. OCR staff needed to determine more specifically who was to be considered handicapped for the purpose of the law and what was to be considered discrimination against them. Memoranda were prepared laying out legal and policy questions on issues including the definition of a handicapped person, how Section 504 applied to employment, what was to be done about architectural barriers, as well as on a number of substantive areas corresponding to agencies within HEW, such as health, higher education, elementary and secondary education, and social services.

First, further explanation of the new definition of "handicapped individual" was needed for the Section 504 regulation. Several definitions were already used in other federal programs; HEW alone used separate definitions for programs in vocational rehabilitation, vocational education, education of children in elementary and secondary schools, and social security disability. Some of this variation may be explained by the tendency of distinct bureaucratic units to prefer their own definitions. More significantly, some physical problems may become handicaps only in particular settings (for example, with respect to employment or education), and definitions can legitimately vary in programs with differing purposes. Thus, OCR staff recommended that

the Section 504 regulation develop yet another definition of handicapped individual.

Another major issue concerned inclusion of poor people, aged people, homosexuals, and drug and alcohol
addicts within the definition of handicapped individuals. An intradepartmental memorandum prepared by
Wodatch discussed the potential inclusion of these various social pariahs.[12] Wodatch felt that neither aged nor
poor people should be covered by Section 504. Aging and
poverty may be contributing factors in the etiology of
various handicapping conditions, and poverty is often a
consequence of disability, but aging and poverty are not
in themselves handicapping conditions. Furthermore,
there was nothing in the legislative history of Section
504 to indicate that Congress intended either aged people or poor people to be included. Wodatch also recommended that homosexuals be excluded from coverage by
Section 504, thus avoiding what would certainly have
been a political brouhaha of the first magnitude. While
some psychiatrists and other professionals consider homosexuality to be rooted in psychopathology and in-
dicative of mental disorder, the American Psychiatric
Association in 1973 had removed homosexuality from its
list of mental disorders. Further, neither legislative history nor traditional use of the term handicap had classi-
fied homosexuality as a handicapping condition.

Using similar logic to opposite effect, Wodatch cited
medical and legal authorities in support of the conclusion that drug and alcohol addictions were diseases in
and of themselves and should be considered disabilities
protected by Section 504. The analysis noted the inclusion of addicts in other federal programs, which define
drug and alcohol addiction as disabilities and include re-
habilitated addicts among their clients. Although inclusion of alcoholics and drug addicts as a group protected
by Section 504 was to be politically controversial in
securing support for the regulation, the legal basis for

69

their inclusion was never successfully challenged. Thus alcoholics and drug addicts who satisfied eligibility requirements could not be discriminated against in federally supported programs as long as their addiction would not interfere with their program participation.

Once the relevant population that was entitled to protection under Section 504 had been identified, a second definition was necessary to specify what constituted discrimination against a qualified handicapped person. The regulation for Section 504 deals with two types of barriers to participation of disabled people that have discriminatory effects—attitudinal barriers and physical barriers.

Stigmatization and attitudinal barriers have significantly limited disabled people's access to the mainstream of American life. For instance, a prospective employer or service provider might feel uncomfortable around disabled persons and therefore tacitly exclude them from programs or employment. Without evidence, an employer or provider might assume that a disabled person might be too handicapped to perform certain tasks or take advantage of a program. Such attitudinal barriers have been and continue to be widespread and institutionalized in many sectors of American society. Section 504 seeks to deal with such discriminatory attitudes just as Titles VI and IX treat similar attitudes that lead to exclusion or differential treatment of blacks, Hispanics, and women. Although disabled individuals are more commonly victims of pity, discomfort, and condescension than the outright hostility that affects some other excluded groups in our society, the remedies for all attitudinal barriers to participation are similar—ensuring that the excluded group be afforded the same rights and opportunities as everyone else.

One way to end discrimination on the basis of some attribute is to ignore that attribute. In other instances further effort is needed; statutes and programs that provide for affirmative action recognize a particular need for compensatory remedies, while working toward the same ultimate goal of eliminating discrimination and giving everyone an equal chance. Equal treatment is of limited use in breaking down some of the exclusionary barriers affecting disabled people. In interpreting Section 504, the HEW regulation held that equal treatment does not constitute lack of discrimination, unlike discrimination on the basis of race or sex prohibited by Title VI and Title IX. [13]

71

The need for accommodations beyond equal treatment was most apparent in the case of architectural barriers to facilities housing federally supported programs. Even if discriminatory attitudes were to change, these physical barriers would still limit the participation of disabled people in many institutional spheres. In a memorandum drafted by the OCR staff several types of physical barriers are described:

> Many barriers are scarcely noticeable to non-handicapped persons. Obviously, an office building which may only be entered by first climbing a flight of stairs is inaccessible to a person in a wheelchair who seeks employment there. But so too is the building where a ramp to the entrance has been constructed, but there are no restroom cubicles wide enough to accommodate a wheelchair. Hallways which have low hanging signs or light fixtures which those with sight can avoid are barriers to the blind; and deaf persons cannot readily negotiate in a building where, when audial warning devices are used, there are no corresponding visual indicators. [14]

Such barriers were prohibited by the Architectural Barriers Act of 1968, but that act applied only to new buildings constructed, leased, or financed by the federal government, not to existing structures. Section 504, while excluding federal facilities, applies to all buildings and facilities used by recipients of federal financial assistance, whether new or previously constructed and whether or not they were built with direct federal financing.

The regulation writers considered three major issues involving architectural barriers—what to do about existing structures, what to do about new construction, and how to handle timetables and waiver provisions to be included in the regulation. The issue entailing the greatest potential expense involved the alteration of existing buildings and facilities to make them accessible to physically handicapped persons. Many recipients of HEW funds, such as colleges and public school systems, use old facilities whose many architectural barriers would be quite costly to remove.

Some approaches to the problem of making existing facilities accessible were easily rejected. Requiring total accessibility of every room of every building would have been too costly and politically unfeasible. Allowing waivers of accessibility requirements for all existing structures would have exempted the vast majority of recipients of federal funds from the regulation for a long time to come and would have drastically limited Section 504's impact. Wodatch and his staff recommended a compromise approach, program accessibility, in which each element of the program or activity but not every facility supported by federal funds would have to be accessible to physically handicapped persons. As long as disabled people could participate in all parts of any given program, they did not need to have access to every room or even every building housing the program.

A program accessibility standard, then, would not necessarily require structural changes. Program access could be provided through accommodations such as moving services or classes to accessible areas, redesigning equipment, assigning aides to handicapped persons, or providing services in the handicapped person's home. The example of a university was offered in Wodatch's memorandum:

> For example, a college or university would not have to make every dormitory or every floor of every dormitory accessible; but it would have to change enough of its dormitories so that housing would be available to all handicapped students who desire to attend the college. Similarly, enough classrooms would have to be made accessible so that handicapped students could not be denied entrance to classes or courses because of the lack of accessible classrooms. . . . Class schedules could be rearranged so that those courses with handicapped students would be taught only in already accessible rooms. . . . In a college library which is housed in an old building in which it would be difficult or impossible to install elevators or lifts, the library could make available personnel on an as needed basis to go to the upper floors and find the materials needed by a handicapped individual.

A stricter standard was proposed for all new construction, since incorporating barrier-free features into new construction requires minimal effort or expense by the architect, builder, and user of a facility. The memo cited a study by the National League of Cities in which barrier-free construction was estimated as adding less than one percent to the total cost of a building. Wodatch recommended that new construction be required to conform to barrier-free standards developed by the American National Standards Institute, a clearinghouse and coordinating body for standards in the United States, whose membership includes trade associations, technical societies, professional groups, consumer organizations, and over one thousand private companies. In 1959, the President's Committee on the Employment of the Handicapped sponsored an ANSI conference, which led to the publication in 1961 of ANSI standards of accessibility for physically handicapped persons. The publication included specifications for ramp construction and gradients, grading of walkways, location of parking spaces, widths of doors, door handle design and pressure, visual and audible signals, and location of elevator controls, light switches, telephones, and water fountains. By the time the regulation for Section 504 was being developed, the standards had been adopted in some version by every state, primarily for the construction of public buildings, and by the federal Architectural and Transportation Barriers Compliance Board.[15]

Finally, Wodatch recommended that, given the flexibility of the program accessibility standard for existing buildings, no waivers should be permitted of the accessibility requirements. Recipients were to be given three years to meet the standards from the effective date of the regulation.

The architectural barriers section later proved to be among the Section 504 regulation's most misunderstood and controversial provisions. A great deal of explanation was necessary to convey the program accessibility concept to recipients of federal funds. Universities in particular, with their traditionally designed campuses and limited discretionary funds, were to complain bitterly about the costs of opening even a portion of their facilities to disabled students. Hospitals, already designed in large part to accommodate individuals with medical problems impairing their mobility, would need to make fewer changes. Because of the diversity of institutional problems in providing access, the OCR staff prepared specific subparts of the regulation dealing with issues in employment, elementary and secondary education, post-secondary education, and health, welfare, and social services.

An underlying but often unacknowledged issue in

the preparation of the regulation for Section 504 was the cost of the implementation of its various provisions. Cost was not directly addressed in the draft regulation and was officially a "nonissue," one whose consideration was felt to be illegitimate by most of the OCR staff, including the key decision-makers, Gerry, Wodatch, and Beckman.

There were three rationales for the general exclusion of cost considerations. The first was the belief that in civil rights law, the cost of ensuring nondiscrimination was, while not exactly irrelevant, an unreasonable excuse for condoning discrimination. This was an extension of the position propounded by OCR and upheld by the federal courts throughout the process of desegregating the schools and other Jim Crow institutions in the South during the 1960s. Southern school districts and political officials had often cited cost as an excuse for not complying with statutory and court-ordered mandates to desegregate. Such arguments had been consistently ruled illegitimate: the very idea of a right is that it should be recognized without view to inconvenience, competing priorities, or disruptive effect.

In practice, however, cost was seen as a legitimate concern in fashioning remedies to discrimination. Thus, the standard of discrimination was to be set regardless of cost, while the determination of how that right would be reached could include consideration of cost. This dual approach was set out in the regulation's preamble:

> The proposed regulation does not take into account the cost or difficulty of eliminating discrimination in establishing the standards for what constitutes discrimination. . . . The Department agrees in principle with the concept that cost or difficulty are appropriate considerations, not in determining what constitutes discrimination, but in fashioning a remedy if a recipient has been found to be discriminating.[16]

75

A second rationale for disregarding the cost to recipients was the belief that the costs involved would not be great, except for those involved in eliminating architectural barriers in existing buildings, which would be one-time costs. Costs, it was argued, could be ignored, and to claim otherwise was felt to be cynical obstruction. Martin Gerry recalled this perspective:

76

> There's a traditional reluctance with civil rights regulations to deal with money. Partly because money was always kind of a red herring in race discrimination issues. It certainly was. There was all this stuff about how expensive it was going to be to eliminate the dual school system. Well of course it saved money. There's less busing than under the dual school system, there are fewer schools. It was all a shell game. Then you had all the rat trap about Title IX. Ohio State was going out of business. The world was going to end, the sky was going to fall, big-time college football was gone. And money got dragged into that constantly. The revenue-producing sports issue in Title IX over-shadowed little things like curriculum content. So there was a growing reluctance [by federal policy-makers] to deal with the issues of money.

Again, this view was in part based on OCR's experience in enforcing Title VI, which in fact had not cost a great deal.[17] The view seemed also to be based on ideological disregard for problems involved in doing the right thing. One OCR staffer, Sally Foley, recalled:

> In our office the party line was that it doesn't cost anything, and I don't know what the hell we think it costs to even build a ramp. We constantly say that it doesn't cost anything. We constantly say the costs are exaggerated, exaggerated by the nasties out there who don't want the handicapped to have access. As though there's some conspiracy out there to say it costs money, to what end, I don't know,

because we never took it to the final degree, that it must be that some people are anti-handicapped. We never said that. I guess we thought they were lazy thinkers, architects gone mad. And sometimes that happened, sometimes architects have abused us, and have said you must have an elevator in this wing when indeed you don't have to. The person could be accommodated in some other way.

The third rationale for disregarding costs was that even if there were sizable costs associated with compliance, they would be outweighed by the benefits involved. This argument was made not only in terms of the intangible benefits to disabled people of greater participation, but also in terms of actual financial benefits. OCR staff believed that eliminating enforced dependency on public charity by allowing disabled people to obtain education, vocational training, and ultimately jobs would lead to decreased welfare costs and increased tax revenues. Thus the long-term benefits of Section 504 would exceed the short-term costs of eliminating barriers to participation.[18]

While disregard of costs was a major tenet of faith within OCR, inevitably some consideration of the financial burden for recipients was made. Requiring program accessibility rather than access to all parts of all facilities is the most important evidence of this, as were the exemptions ultimately granted small service providers. However, the Office for Civil Rights generally held to the doctrine that cost was not a valid excuse for discrimination against disabled people.[19]

Once the substantive areas had been identified, each area was assigned to one or more OCR staff members, who were responsible for preparing memoranda outlining the key issues for decisions. After initial review and revision by John Wodatch and his deputy, Ann Beckman, the memoranda were circulated to the HEW operating agencies responsible for the programs covered in the regulation. Formal approval was sought from program administrators and from staff agencies such as the Office of General Counsel, the legislative liaison office, and the Office of the Assistant Secretary for Planning and Evaluation. Wodatch estimates that about twenty people within HEW reviewed one or more memoranda analyzing issues for the regulation.

Once comments were returned and drafts for the various sections of the regulation were written on the basis of the comments, a full first draft was prepared. Finished by the end of April 1975, the draft was largely the work of Wodatch and Beckman, with assistance from their staff and from OCR top management. The draft was circulated to HEW line and staff agencies for additional comments and, ultimately, approval. In cases where consensus could not be reached, issues were brought to the HEW secretary, Caspar Weinberger (and later David Mathews), for resolution. The draft was also reviewed by congressional staff, notably Lisa Walker in the Senate and Jack Duncan in the House. As Wodatch commented, the benefits of such an extensive review before finalizing the proposed regulation were many:

> It was a very helpful process in terms of getting a feel for how the regulation would affect different kinds of recipients, because the people in HEW know their programs fairly well, and could say, that's fine, but it's going to have this kind of impact on these kind of providers and it will do X, Y, and Z, and you could sit around the table in a fairly noncombative way and say, well, what we're really interested in is ensuring that handicapped people can participate. How can they participate in this kind of program without doing great damage? And it was that sort of give and take.

Wodatch felt that this give and take meant a balanced regulation and that the review was typical for complex regulations coming out of large agencies. In addition to providing OCR with suggestions and criticisms, the process served to inform and educate the various program people and top agency management about Section 504, although the high rate of turnover in top HEW positions meant a continuing need for explication.

As the review continued, new considerations were raised, particularly in the health area, and several minor revisions in the draft regulation were made. However, the basic approach of the regulation did not change. Ultimately, all of the concerns of the HEW agencies were addressed and their approval was obtained.

While the regulation was being prepared, only limited contact was made with groups outside HEW, although congressional staff were consulted periodically. OCR staff had made few attempts to contact representatives of federal fund recipients who would be affected by the regulation, such as universities, hospitals, or local governments. Wodatch felt that the officials within the department who were involved in the various substantive programs could adequately represent the views of the recipients. Office of Education staff served as proxies for the universities, Medicaid/Medicare staff for the hospitals, and so on.

Contacts made with disabled individuals typically were on an informal, individual basis rather than through formal organizational contacts. Most disabled individuals were consulted through a loose network of personal ties among OCR staff, congressional staff, civil rights activists, and disability rights advocates. The involvement of disabled individuals was sought more for information than for advocacy purposes. Since the staff of the Office for Civil Rights had background in civil rights but little knowledge of disabilities, they needed to draw upon people who were knowledgeable and thoughtful about discrimination on the basis of handicap. The perspectives and experiences of disabled individuals were tapped in developing the regulation and in the self-education of the regulation writers. As a byproduct, gradually, informally, the word got out to disability advocates that Section 504 existed and that it was important. Formal involvement by organized groups did not take place until the proposed regulation had already been drafted, in part because of the limited organizational capacities of most disability organizations. However, the ability of disability rights organizations to influence policy decisions was to grow.

80

Once the regulation was drafted and approved by the various agencies within the HEW, the approval of the secretary was needed. When approved, the regulation would be published in proposed form for comments. A great deal of work had been done and most of the possible objections to the regulation had already been anticipated, so secretarial approval should have been fairly routine, particularly since Secretary Weinberger had been kept informed as the draft regulation was finalized and had been called on to resolve several disagreements about its content.

At this point, however, political conflict, which had been generally absent from the early stages of the regulation's development, began to appear. It had taken about twenty months from the passage of the Rehabilitation Act in 1973 for the technical process of drafting and revising the regulation for Section 504 to be completed. The regulation was submitted to Secretary Weinberger in July 1975, with the recommendation that it be published in proposed form at that time. It was to take nearly two additional years for the regulation finally to be put into effect. But the initial consideration of the Section 504 regulation had been on technical civil rights grounds, which were insulated from politics. This insulation allowed the participants to follow their professional and political ideologies to craft a very strong regulation. By the time the regulation became exposed to direct interest group politics outside of HEW, its nature had already become institutionalized to such an extent that those opposed to it were hard-pressed to change the regulation in major ways.

5 Advocacy and the HEW Regulation

Until 1974, there had been little or no attempt by the various organizations of disabled people to join together in attempts to influence public policy. For years several groups with active organizations, notably blind people, deaf people, and disabled veterans, had sought to influence federal legislation. Despite their related objectives, however, they had not tried to affiliate in any formal way. The annual meetings of the President's Committee on Employment of the Handicapped provided a forum for communication among some of the younger, more militant disability rights activists. Several remained in contact in the times between meetings, and an evolving network helped to organize the demonstrations against the presidential vetoes of the Rehabilitation Act in 1972 and 1973. The demonstrations, in turn, helped to strengthen personal and organizational ties among disabled activists.

Coalition-Building by Advocates

This loose network was formed into an organization at the 1974 PCEH meeting. Judy Heumann and Eunice Fiorito of Disabled in Action of New York, along with others, organized workshop sessions that met in the middle of the lobby of the conference hotel, the Washington Hilton. About 150 people got together to discuss discrimination issues not included in the formal program, and this group organized a cross-disability organization, the American Coalition of Citizens with Disabilities (ACCD), which linked several of the existing groups while retaining the autonomy of each constituent association.

A steering committee was formed, and ACCD held its first formal meeting the following year, at the 1975 PCEH meeting. Bylaws were adopted, and nineteen organizations joined the coalition, including representatives of blind, deaf, and orthopedically impaired persons. A board of directors was elected, including representatives of the major disabilities and organizations involved. Eunice Fiorito, who was elected as the first president, coordinated the coalition's activities out of her New York office. A small office was also opened in Washington and staffed by volunteers.

ACCD had no paid staff in its first year and a very limited budget, so its first task was to raise money for its own operation. Funds were sought in order to monitor legislation, lobby, and keep member organizations informed about events in Washington. (Established organizations representing disabled veterans, deaf people, and blind people, already had Washington offices.) Board meetings were held around the country to drum up support within the disability community. Rather than rely exclusively on the meager financial and in-kind support available from its membership, the ACCD board decided to seek federal funds. They first approached Andrew Adams, commissioner of the RSA. With his help, the board prepared a grant proposal and submitted it to RSA, asking support for "a feasibility study to develop a national model for cross-disability communication and cooperation." Fiorito recalls:

> It was a study to determine the ability to establish a coalition for communication, coordination, and some other dumb thing. Anyhow, it was a pretext to get some money

83

> for the coalition to get going. . . . All I knew was that I had
> to get the thing off the ground, and that if we didn't get
> money, we weren't going anywhere.

RSA approved a one-year grant, starting in September
1976.

Until the spring of 1975, most leaders of disability organizations, including ACCD, were not aware of Section

84   504 and the regulations being developed for it. (One important exception was the National Federation of the
Blind.) In 1975, OCR began to consult with several established disability organizations, including the Easter
Seal Society and the United Cerebral Palsy Association.
That year was also a time of developing contacts among
disability advocates, congressional staff, and several
Washington civil rights groups. Through this evolving
network, Section 504 became more widely known outside of HEW. Key members of the network included
Judy Heumann and Ann Rosewater.

Heumann, founder and first president of Disabled in
Action and an organizer of ACCD, had left her teaching
position in New York City and gone to graduate school
at the University of California, Berkeley. As part of her
degree program, she went to work as an intern for Lisa
Walker in Washington, where she was involved with the
drafting of the Education for All Handicapped Children
Act, P.L. 94-142. She also came into contact with representatives of Washington civil rights organizations, including Ann Rosewater of the Children's Defense Fund
and Cynthia Brown of the Lawyers Committee on Civil
Rights, who was later appointed assistant secretary of
education for civil rights by Jimmy Carter. Rosewater
had been project director for a CDF study of children excluded from public schools, which had, among other
things, examined the relationship between racial discrimination and the labeling of children as mentally retarded. The staff for the study included people previously working at the HEW Office for Civil Rights and

drew heavily on data collected by OCR in a survey it had conducted on public school desegregation. In late 1974 and early 1975, after publication of the study, Rosewater was active in trying to prevent the misclassification of minority children in special education. She met with Nik Edes, Lisa Walker, and Judy Heumann to try to get protections against prejudicial misclassification included in P.L. 94-142. Having learned about Section 504 from them, Rosewater subsequently met with John Wodatch, Ann Beckman, and Bud Keith of OCR to urge that similar protections be included in the Section 504 regulation. At the same time, Rosewater was attempting to organize coalitions of advocacy groups. She was interested in identifying issues that affected poor people and racial minorities but also involved other groups. She saw Section 504 as a potential link between groups traditionally interested in civil rights and disability advocates, and worked to get disability groups interested in the section.

In late 1975, Judy Heumann returned to Berkeley to join the staff of the Center for Independent Living. As the result of contacts with Heumann and CIL's director Ed Roberts, Rosewater was invited to give workshops on civil rights at several conferences of disability advocates on the west coast. At these meetings, Rosewater talked about the potential of Section 504 and urged that disabled groups and individuals get involved in the rulemaking. Consequently, ACCD and other organizations began to get interested in Section 504 when the draft regulation was completed and submitted to Secretary Weinberger for approval. Rosewater and Heumann helped to build links between OCR staff and some of the disability community's leadership, as OCR sought information about disability, and disability organizations educated themselves about the politics of disability at the national level. Disability organizations, particularly ACCD, were to have an important impact on the final substance of the regulation for Section 504.

The movement of disabled people was influenced in

important ways by the federal government in the 1970s. The President's Committee for Employment of the Handicapped provided a setting for organization. The growing vocational rehabilitation program, the developmental disabilities program, and other programs serving disabled people provided a great deal of money that enabled the development of policy and research centers and of advocacy organizations. Many organizations representing disabled people received a major portion of their operating expenses from various wings of HEW in the form of training grants, technical assistance contracts, and funds for demonstration projects.

Such support was to rebound upon the federal government. ACCD, for example, received seed money from HEW and subsequently organized a series of demonstrations in HEW offices and led a concerted effort to influence HEW policies. A number of organizations within the disability rights movement tried to shape federal policy while drawing much of their financial support from the federal government. Furthermore, a number of individuals involved in creating disability rights policy alternated between jobs in government and the private and/or public interest sector. Government officials became private consultants to advocacy groups while advocates joined congressional staffs or HEW agencies. In addition to staff and funds, information about programs and policy concepts were also constantly being borrowed or transmitted across a network of government agencies and nongovernmental organizations.

Publishing the Regulation

By the summer of 1975, a final draft of the proposed regulation for Section 504 had been prepared by John Wodatch and his staff in the HEW Office for Civil Rights. When regulations are developed by a federal agency, they are typically published in the *Federal Register*, an official publication that serves as a means of informing the public of decisions made within the executive branch. Usually regulations are published in the form of proposed regulations. After public comments are received, the proposed rule is revised and republished as a final regulation, which has the force of law. In the Department of Health, Education, and Welfare, regulations such as the one for Section 504 required the approval of the secretary in order for the publication cycle to begin. On July 23, 1975, a draft of the proposed regulation and an explanatory preamble to be published along with it had been submitted to Secretary Weinberger for approval by Martin Gerry, then acting director of OCR. Shortly thereafter, however, David Mathews replaced Weinberger as secretary of the Department of Health, Education, and Welfare.

Secretary Mathews developed a reputation among HEW staff as a cautious and indecisive man who tended to be more philosophical than pragmatic in running the department. Martin Gerry recalled the secretary's "profound concern about the whole process of government." Faced with difficult and complex regulatory issues, Mathews might ask whether regulations should be issued at all. This caution was frustrating to those who saw the role of government in activist terms. For example, Nik Edes of Senator Williams's staff characterized the secretary as "someone who did not run his department. He was [merely] a person who sat in the Secretary's office."

When Mathews took office, he was briefed about the Section 504 regulation and became quite interested in some of the issues involved. He was particularly concerned with the overall impact of the regulation on disabled people and the existing system of services for them. Further, Mathews questioned the appropriateness of including alcoholics, drug addicts, and mentally ill persons within the definition of a handicapped person. Martin Gerry characterized the secretary's reaction to the regulation:

> His basic inclination was to just let the whole thing go away; he didn't want to put out regulations. He certainly had a more-or-less charity mentality toward disabled people, not in the malevolent sense but in a paternalistic sense. He really just didn't get the idea that these were rights and that you weren't really talking about nice things to do for Easter Seal children. Then when we got to alcoholics and drug addicts, he really flipped out. These were obviously derelicts, and they were so far from Easter Seal children, things had truly run amok. . . .
>
> His main concern was that by giving in to junkies and addicts and all those other people and doing too much, we were going to screw up the basic charity system. I think he sincerely believed that the net effect of all this might be to really injure handicapped people, and take away from them some of the benefits they had already won over the years.

John Wodatch explained Mathews's hesitancy about the regulation:

> I think it scared him. I mean it was a major change in society. And I don't think he trusted the bureaucracy that produced it. And he didn't like the advice he was getting, he didn't want to sign it. He didn't like the fact that alcoholics and drug addicts were covered, neither did Califano. He saw major changes, he saw it as coming out of a liberal OCR, he just didn't want to do it.

Despite his discomfort, the secretary did not seek specific changes in the draft. According to Martin Gerry, he was primarily interested in its general approach: "He [did not have] a lot of concrete ideas about how [the regulation] should be written. He really had more concerns about things that might happen, or the whole legitimacy of the regulation-writing process. We didn't have many fights over content." Secretary Mathews's response to the draft regulation was shared by the head of the agency within HEW, traditionally concerned with programs for disabled people, the Rehabilitative Services Administration. In a memorandum responding to the completed draft, Dr. Andrew Adams, the commissioner of rehabilitative services, had written:

> Because of the tone, the very broad scope and reach of the draft regulations, it is our view that without addition of some time-phased and comparable provisions for implementation (allowing more time for compliance), there might well be a backlash reaction against the population the law aims to benefit. . . .
>
> We would prefer an approach somewhat more from the advocacy and affirmative action point of view and less from the enforcement of compliance point of view. We would also prefer less comprehensiveness and specificity.[1]

Mathews did not directly oppose the Section 504 regulation by seeking changes in the statute. Rather, he demanded further analysis of the draft regulation, and thus delayed publishing it in proposed form. One particular source of delay was the development of an "inflation impact statement."

Executive Order 11821 required that any proposal by a federal agency involving expenditures of over $100 million include an assessment of its impact on inflation.[2] In his transmittal memorandum to the secretary accompanying the draft regulation, Martin Gerry had stated that the Section 504 regulation would probably exceed the $100 million threshold, and that an inflation impact statement would be necessary.[3] He reported that analysis for the statement had been begun and that it would be completed before the regulation would be published in its final form.

Mathews seized upon the need for such a statement

as a rationale for delaying publication of the draft regulation. He asked for and received a draft inflation impact statement prepared by staff from OCR and the Office of the Assistant Secretary for Planning and Evaluation by the end of August 1975. The forty-eight-page draft concluded that the major costs of implementing the regulation would be for modifying existing buildings and for additional services in elementary and secondary education. It argued that these costs were justified by the benefits to disabled persons and by increased revenues to state and federal government as disabled people entered employment, paid taxes, and needed fewer government services.

Mathews considered this in-house analysis inadequate, so a more extensive cost/benefit evaluation of the regulation was commissioned from a private consulting firm, the Public Interest Institute. During the fall of 1975 and the winter of 1976 this analysis was prepared by Dave M. O'Neill, who worked closely with Ann Beckman and Ed Lynch of the Office for Civil Rights staff.

The inflation impact statement was the first attempt to confront the cost of implementing the Section 504 regulation directly by examining the combined effects of all of its provisions. For each subpart of the regulation, the number and magnitude of required changes were estimated, along with specific (but clearly hypothetical) cost figures. O'Neill estimated that the only major costs of implementing Section 504 would be to increase accessibility in elementary and secondary education ($2.3 billion), while there would be financial benefits from providing access in employment ($0.5 billion) and elementary and secondary education ($1.5 billion). He calculated the overall benefit as $0.3 billion.[4] (A summary of the major findings of the inflation impact statement is provided in Appendix D.) O'Neill's overall conclusion was: "The benefits forthcoming (psychic as well as pecuniary) provide a substantial offset to the costs that will be incurred. The costs involved will not be as great as is widely thought and the compelling situation of some of the handicapped persons involved tips the balance in favor of proceeding with immediate implementation of the regulation."[5]

Since this conclusion was virtually the same as the earlier in-house statement and generally in agreement with the stance taken by OCR all along, O'Neill's analysis had little substantive impact on the draft regulation. Advocates within OCR consistently treated the cost of implementation as a nonissue, and they saw the inflation impact statement essentially as an excuse for delay rather than a consideration of important substantive issues. Even those with serious questions about the regulation within the department, such as Secretary Mathews, were more concerned about the social consequences of the broad definition of disability and the expanded role of the federal bureaucracy in the operation of recipients than they were about cost. The debate about cost that developed later did not center to any significant extent on the findings of O'Neill's analysis. The inflation impact statement served primarily as a symbolic reassertion of the utility of the regulation.

O'Neill's report was submitted in February 1976, six months after the shorter in-house statement had been completed. With the impact statement prepared, there were no formal barriers to publication of the draft regulation other than obtaining the approval of Secretary Mathews. Gerry again submitted the draft regulation to the secretary on March 11, 1976, and urged its publication, but Mathews still would not take official action, although he never gave an official rationale for failing to do so.

By the spring of 1976, the informal relationships that had grown up between OCR staff and disability advocates became a mechanism for both to exert pressure on the secretary to act. Information was relayed from advocates within the Office for Civil Rights to those outside of it, who were in a position to try to influence Secretary Mathews.

One outside source of advocacy was Congress. The congressional staff responsible for Section 504 urged their patrons to pressure HEW to issue the regulation. Senators Williams and Randolph, who chaired the Senate Committee on Labor and Public Welfare and its Subcommittee on the Handicapped respectively, held public oversight hearings in May of 1976 to monitor the implementation of Sections 501, 503, and 504. At the hearings, Martin Gerry and John Wodatch were lectured by Senator Williams about the need for prompt action of the Section 504 regulation and questioned about the delay in publication. In response, the OCR officials did not mention the reluctance of their secretary to approve publication of the proposed regulation nor the fact that a draft of the regulation had been completed for over a year. Rather, they cited the lack of legislative history and the complexity of defining who would be considered protected by Section 504 and what was to constitute discrimination against them. They also cited an insufficient number of staff.[6] Gerry promised the senators that the proposed regulation would soon be issued, that public comments would be widely solicited, and that enforcement would proceed vigorously. The encouragement of Senators Williams and Randolph no doubt hastened action by Secretary Mathews.

In addition to congressional contacts, other networks were used to spread the word about the recalcitrance of the secretary. After the internal review of the draft regulation, a variety of outside public agencies, organizations of disabled people, and recipients of federal funds had been consulted. More than sixty such organizations were contacted in 1975 and early 1976. In the course of these consultations, relationships and even friendships developed between OCR staff and organizational representatives. Such relationships were particularly close for the Washington representatives of disability rights groups such as ACCD, the American Council for the Blind, and the National Association of the Deaf. The OCR staff consulted with disability rights advocates more and more frequently, while at the same time several disability organizations, particularly ACCD, were lobbying Congress and the executive branch about their concerns. John Wodatch and Ann Beckman became involved with these groups, as did OCR staff members Ed Lynch and Bud Keith, who were specifically assigned to maintain liaisons outside of HEW.

These contacts culminated in a demonstration by a number of disabled leaders in David Mathews's office in the spring of 1976. The activists demanded immediate publication of the draft regulation without any weakening of its provisions. According to Eunice Fiorito, the demonstration was encouraged by Wodatch and Gerry. The disability activists were treated cordially but in what they considered to be a patronizing manner. Their response was to threaten to picket the upcoming 1976 Republican Convention. Shortly following the demonstration, the regulation was published in the *Federal Register*.

The standard procedure for issuing federal regulations is that they first be published in proposed form, in a notice of proposed rulemaking (NPRM). Secretary Mathews, however, decided that the regulation for Section 504 should first be published in an even more tentative form. In what appears to have been an unprecedented procedure, the draft regulation was published as a notice of intent to publish proposed rules (NIPRM) on May 17, 1976. In the preamble to the NIPRM, the following rationale was given:

> The most important problem which has hindered the development of the regulation is the constant need to weigh competing equities while resolving complex issues. Thus,

93

while we recognize that the statute creates individual rights, the statute is ambiguous as to the specific scope of these rights. Implicit in this situation is the need to assess carefully the overall impact of a particular requirement both on the persons protected by the statute and regulated by it.

Since it appears to be the case that the implications of this legislation have not been elaborated before the general public in sufficient detail, it seems appropriate, before issuing a Notice of Proposed Rulemaking, to solicit public comment on certain key issues which any proposed regulation would, in all likelihood, address.[7]

Weighing the rights of disabled people against the impact on recipients of federal funds in this way suggests a reluctance to accept the civil rights emphasis that the OCR staff had made in developing the Section 504 regulation.

A thirty-day period was allowed for individuals and organizations to provide comments on the draft regulation. OCR received over three hundred written comments, and the staff held public meetings in ten cities around the country. Comments were received from both disability rights advocates and from recipients of federal funds. For the most part, the advocates supported the regulation, with questions about the propriety of balancing the rights of disabled people against the cost and difficulty of compliance. Advocates also questioned allowing affected recipients extended periods of time to meet the regulation's requirements. Recipients of federal funds objected to the financial burden of compliance and sought relief from that burden through waivers or at least through an extended phasing-in period for compliance. Colleges and universities provided the largest number of comments and were particularly concerned about the cost of modifying architectural barriers and providing auxiliary aids.

A new draft regulation published on July 16 as a notice of proposed rulemaking was very similar to the original draft published in the notice of intent. The OCR staff retained drug addicts and alcoholics in the definition of handicapped individual despite protests about their inclusion. OCR further insisted that cost and difficulty of compliance were not valid considerations in determining what practices constitute discrimination, but that costs could be relevant in determining remedies for discrimination.

Some changes were made to strengthen the regulation, but most were minor technical or clarifying changes. Perhaps the most important was the decision to not exclude Medicaid providers from the requirements of Section 504. (Under Medicaid, health care for low-income individuals is subsidized by federal and state funds in a state-administered program.) In the original notice of intent, those health care providers whose only involvement with federal funds was participation in Medicaid were exempted from the accessibility requirements as a class. Due to objections raised in the comments, this exclusion was subsequently deleted, and physicians and others providing Medicaid-reimbursed services were made subject to the Section 504 requirements. However, concern about the effects of the requirements on small recipients in general led OCR to add a provision exempting all federal fund recipients with fifteen or fewer employees from several grievance and notification requirements.

Following publication of the NPRM, the OCR staff devoted considerable effort to publicizing the proposed regulation and soliciting comments from recipients, disabled people, and their representatives. A sixty-day comment period, until September 14, was permitted for the submission of such comments. After that period, work was to begin on the final revision of the regulation.

Frustrated by delays, disability advocates sought to hasten this prolonged administrative process through the courts. In June 1975, James Cherry and the Action

League for Physically Handicapped Adults filed suit in federal court to force the issuance of regulations for Section 504. In July 1976, Judge John Smith of the U.S. District Court for the District of Columbia ruled that the secretary of HEW was required to issue the regulation, although not by a given date.[8] The attorneys for the plaintiffs in the case, known as *Cherry v. Mathews*, all worked for the Institute for Public Interest Representation, which was connected to the Georgetown University Law School and served as a center for disability rights advocacy throughout the Section 504 implementation process.

A community had grown up among the advocates in Washington seeking a strong and effective regulation, including disability groups and public interest lawyers with more general advocacy concerns. Disability advocates began to meet regularly in Washington to compare notes, develop strategies, and divide up the various tasks of lobbying. Durwood McDaniel, of the American Council of the Blind, recalls that fifteen or twenty people began meeting at the ACB office shortly after the proposed rules were published. Among them were several individuals from the government, including Lisa Walker from the Senate committee and one or two OCR staff members. Organizations were assigned responsibilities for analyzing various sections of the regulation. Positions on issues were debated and agreements were reached on public stances. The complexity of lobbying for a strong regulation helped to knit these groups together into a network that served to share information and coordinate actions.

At the same time that the disability advocates were organizing to influence the regulations, the Office for Civil Rights was seeking additional feedback on the regulation. In August, "town meetings" were scheduled in twenty-two different cities across the country to discuss the proposed regulation. In the fall of 1976, a series of additional meetings were held with recipients and disabled representatives to get further comments. Throughout the public comment period, the position of the disability community remained consistent. They maintained that Section 504 was a simple prohibition of discrimination and that there was nothing in it which would permit deviation from its strict application. They were suspicious of recipients and sought to limit any flexibility for recipient institutions in interpreting the regulation. A representative comment submitted to OCR was from the National Center for Law and the Handicapped:

> An attempt to create an equation on the one side of which are persons sought to be protected by the statute and on the other side of which are the persons to be regulated by it will do nothing to right the imbalance the Congress sought to redress by enacting Section 504. It is as if the Department were saying that it will lean neither toward discrimination on the one hand nor toward non-discrimination on the other. Faithful execution of the statute requires that *everything* in the regulations point toward the timely achievement of non-discrimination. . . .The third area of difficulty involves wording that might prove to serve as a series of sanctuaries for persons who wish to evade their responsibilities under the statute. In particular we are concerned about the invitations to claim hardship that would result in unwarranted delays and in the segregation of the handicapped.[9]

Disabled representatives had become informally involved in the development of the regulation before its publication. They had developed working relationships with staff in the Office of Civil Rights and knew the background for what was included in the draft and why. Most recipients of federal funds did not have these advantages in commenting on the proposed regulation. Their representatives had no particular reason to monitor legislation and administrative actions affecting disabled persons. Prior to the publication of the draft regulation, most recipients were unaware that they might be faced with substantial requirements to provide access to disabled persons. The Office for Civil Rights had made little effort to notify recipients about Section 504 until the summer of 1976. When first contacts were made, many recipients did not grasp the implications of the regulation. John Wodatch recalls:

> At each one of these first town meetings in each town we tried to invite representatives of recipients in that area to the meetings. So that was the first big attempt to draw them in. At that point we sent out copies of the notice of intent to a lot of recipients, but even that didn't get their attention. You had to really go out and sort of shake them and say, please come and participate in this. . . . We got a lot of comments, but not as much as you would have thought. In those days, though, no one knew about 504. No one thought a lot about handicapped issues, and so it was somewhat new and it didn't make a lot of sense to people who hadn't thought a lot about it.

Overall, the responses of recipients ranged from apathy to panic to support. In most cases, recipients and their representatives argued for greater flexibility in meeting requirements, for more extended timetables, and for the opportunity to work out problems themselves on a case-by-case basis without intrusion from Washington. There was a great deal of concern with the costs of compliance, particularly with the removal of architectural barriers. In no case was the concept of equal opportunity for disabled persons questioned, but the approach of the regulation was often questioned. A representative comment was that of the National Association of State Universities and Land-Grant Colleges:

> You will find the main theme of our response to be flexibility, as institutions need flexibility in order to respond on

a case by case basis to the needs of handicapped individuals. Also, academic matters *must* remain the responsibility of individual institutions so long as no discrimination is shown. . . .

A very important factor that may have been missed in the thrust of these guidelines is that the concern of most handicapped students and employees, in our experience, has been to assure that the institutions will meet specific needs when requested, not that they will provide an all-enveloping system that will create an unwanted psychology and dependency in these individuals as being in a handicapped (protected) group.[10]

A similar position was taken by the American Council on Education (ACE), which served as a leader of recipients in higher education. ACE, which is an association of over 1,300 colleges and universities and 172 national and regional education associations, was the most vehement voice opposing the regulation in its published form. In comments on the regulation, Staff Counsel Sheldon Steinbach wrote:

The higher education community reiterates its position that, in spite of any discriminatory practices that may exist, the case had not been made to support the proposition that the proposed extensive federal regulatory scheme is essential to secure the education rights of handicapped students. If prior experience with such all-embracing antidiscrimination programs is considered, one could reasonably predict that the end result will be sheaves of unread, unnecessary paper, uneven and inconsistent enforcement by federal field personnel, assumption of antagonistic postures by various affected groups and persons, expenditure of scarce institutional resources on the technicalities of compliance, a staggering backlog of complaints, and the diversion of administration and faculty talent from the more basic continuing goal of fashioning innovative and productive means to aiding handicapped individuals in a manner that promotes real progress.

... In order to achieve the purpose of Section 504, it does not seem essential to have massive, costly modifications and additions to facilities in anticipation of the presence of handicapped individuals on campus. It would seem sufficient to meet the statutory mandate for the regulations to impose an obligation on institutions, to make reasonable accommodation to the handicaps of those individuals who make application for employment or admissions, and those who appear on campus as employees or students. ...

It is readily apparent that the implementation of the regulatory scheme dictated by Section 504 will cause institutions to incur substantial expenditures. While the higher education community stands ready to make the necessary financial commitment to fulfill its responsibilities as federal grantees and contractors, it is essential that these regulations be scrutinized so as to ensure, to the fullest extent possible that the data sought and institutional changes dictated are vital to fulfill the legislative mandate imposed by Section 504. In times of scarce institutional resources each dollar of funds directed toward compliance with a federally mandated program diverts such monies from the instructional purposes which is [sic] the primary function of our colleges and universities.[11]

Some institutions wrote letters of protest about the regulation to Secretary Mathews and to President Ford. However, while institutions did try to influence the process of regulation development, there was no organized attempt to halt the process altogether by having Section 504 amended.

On the whole, the Office for Civil Rights staff were not very sympathetic to the objections raised by recipients. Martin Gerry characterized the response by higher education with some degree of sarcasm:

The reactions to the proposed regulations were quite interesting, I think. The main screaming and yelling was done by the higher education institutions, and that's interesting, because the basic thrust of the regulations is much less intrusive to higher education than it is to elementary and secondary, or even to employment. And I have the feeling that, for whatever reasons, the American Council on Education and its disciples, minions would be the more pejorative term, decided to take on the handicapped as the best political place to make their overregulation fight. . . . At the time, the big issues were money and the big fraud was they're going to make us tear down our universities, and we're already going into economic distress.

All through the summer and much of the fall, meetings were held with various parties affected by the regulation. There were contacts with public officials' organizations, including the National League of Cities, the National Governors Association, and the U.S. Conference of Mayors. Other recipient organizations consulted included the American Hospital Association, the National Association for State Directors of Special Education, the Council for Exceptional Children (which represents special education teachers and other professionals), and several higher education groups, including the National Association of College and University Business Officers (NACUBO) and the College and University Personnel Association (CUPA).

The OCR staff met with recipients and with disabled people and their advocates on the various subparts of the regulation. The disability groups developed a party line among themselves. Using their newly created network, they worked out differences beforehand and established what they were willing to accept in the way of compromises. Prominent participants in the network included Frank Bowe, executive director of ACCD; Deborah Kaplan, director of the Disability Rights Center, a Nader-founded organization; Reese Robrahn of the American Council of the Blind; and Daniel Yohalem from the Children's Defense Fund.

Final Consideration

By early fall of 1976, many organizations and individuals around the country had learned about Section 504 and the proposed regulation. The volume of comments led OCR to extend its comment period to October 14. By that time, over 850 written comments had been received in response to the proposed rules. OCR staff analyzed the comments, grouping them into fourteen general issue areas. Most of these were considered to be minor or clearcut, but four were referred to the secretary for resolution—the inclusion of alcoholics and drug addicts, the modifications to be required of existing buildings, the role to be played by state agencies, and the applicability of minimum wage laws to institutionalized persons.

OCR staff submitted analyses of these issues to Secretary Mathews on December 1, and by early January 1977 final revisions had been made to reflect his concerns. Requirements for the coverage of alcoholics and drug addicts and program accessibility were retained. State agencies were to be explicitly required to inform local agencies of their responsibilities under Section 504 and to monitor and evaluate local agency compliance. Federally financed institutions were to be required to pay a "fair" stipend to disabled workers, but that stipend did not need to be the legal minimum wage.

On January 10, Martin Gerry submitted the final revised regulation to Secretary Mathews for his approval and final publication. Under normal circumstances, the regulation would then have been signed and published. However, with President Ford's loss to Jimmy Carter in the previous November's election, Mathews's tenure was drawing to a close and he apparently did not want to approve a regulation with so many controversial implications for recipients of federal funds.[12] However, on January 18, two days before he left office, Secretary Mathews did act on the regulation for Section 504, but not to sign it. To the surprise of everyone involved, he sent the final regulation to the Senate Committee on Labor and Public Welfare for its review. In a letter to committee chair Harrison Williams, Mathews stated that the language of Section 504 was unclear and sought acknowledgment that his department had followed congressional intent.[13] The secretary's action was seen by OCR staff, disability advocates, and many in Congress as a final stalling tactic. In some instances Congress had, in enacting statutes, specifically mandated a congressional review of regulations before they went into effect. In the absence of such a specific request, however, the issuance of regulations was the responsibility of the executive branch, and Mathews's action was unprecedented.

103

Advocates sought to block Mathews through the courts. On the same day the secretary sent the regulation to Senator Williams, the federal district court that was hearing *Cherry v. Mathews* issued a restraining order on motion of the plaintiffs directing the secretary to cease further delay in issuing the regulation. On January 19, that order was stayed by the U.S. Court of Appeals until the government's case could be heard.

One day later, on January 20, the Carter administration took office and Joseph Califano became secretary of HEW–designate. Since the legal issue of the propriety of sending the regulation to Congress had become moot, Congress never formally responded. It had been over three years since the Rehabilitation Act of 1973 had been passed, and the question of whether the regulation should be approved had still not been resolved.

When President Jimmy Carter took office on January 20, 1977, he had already committed himself to a position on the regulation for Section 504. Eunice Fiorito and another advocate, David Moss, had worked on Carter's campaign, co-chairing the Disabled Community for Carter-Mondale Committee, and had drafted a position paper for Carter on disability rights that he used as the basis for a speech in Warm Springs, Georgia, on September 6, 1976. In this speech, Carter noted that

> Section 504 prohibits discrimination against disabled citizens by recipients of federal financial assistance. These are fine in theory, but they will mean very little until an administration in full accord with their spirit stands behind the law. No administration that really cared about disabled citizens would spend three years trying to avoid enforcing Section 504. No compassionate administration would force disabled consumers to take it to court before it would enforce the law.[14]

Section 504 was hardly a central campaign issue, but Jimmy Carter had put himself on record in favor of prompt approval of a regulation for Section 504. Disabled advocates continued their involvment with the Carter staff after the election, and four ACCD representatives worked on the pre-inauguration transition team.

Carter appointed Joseph Califano as secretary of HEW. A prominent Washington attorney and former aide to President Lyndon Johnson, Califano was known as a liberal on many issues and for his involvement with the Great Society programs of the Johnson years. On his first day in office, Califano received a hand-delivered letter from ACCD and twelve other groups reviewing the history of the Section 504 rulemaking and urging immediate approval of the regulation.

Califano was briefed on the substantive issues involved in the regulation. After the election, OCR Director Martin Gerry was replaced by David Tatel, but responsibility for the Section 504 regulation remained with John Wodatch. A memorandum prepared by Wodatch's OCR staff had listed four possible courses of action to resolve the dispute over publication of a final Section 504 regulation: to seek a response from Congress

104

about the appropriateness of the regulation, as Mathews had done; to review the regulation and have it redrafted; to sign the regulation as it had been submitted on January 10; or to sign the regulation as an "interim" regulation to be reviewed later. The OCR staff recommended immediate signature of the regulation in either final or interim form. The same recommendation was made by Califano's aide, Peter Libassi.

Califano disagreed. Instead he decided to have the regulation studied, with the goals of examining substantive issues and of rewriting the regulation in a shorter, more simplified form. He delegated this study to Libassi, whom he had appointed to be his general counsel. As the first director of the Office of Civil Rights when it was created in the Johnson administration, Libassi had extensive experience in civil rights but none specifically related to the civil rights of disabled people.[15]

Just as there were new figures at HEW, there was new leadership in the disabled community. With the grant from the RSA, the American Coalition of Citizens with Disabilities was able to open a permanent Washington office and hire a full-time salaried executive director, Frank Bowe, an educational psychologist from New York University, who was appointed in September 1976. Bowe's presence allowed ACCD to monitor the rulemaking process for Section 504 and other federal policies affecting disabled people much more closely. From January through May of 1977, Bowe and the other ACCD office staff did little else but seek approval of the Section 504 regulation in the version that had been on Secretary Mathews's desk when he left office.

According to Peter Libassi, he and Califano were initially skeptical about the regulation. They saw the regulation as a reflection of the demands of the disabled groups without appreciation of the political and financial implications:

Now the regulation that was on our desk to be signed, in my judgment, reflected a don't care attitude by the previous political leadership of the department, because they were leaving. And so it was a staff document. It was the fulfillment and embodiment of what everybody could have ever wanted to protect the rights of the handicapped, without regard to any balancing or conflicting problems. The law was bad enough, in the sense of just saying stop all discrimination against the handicapped. And the regulations, then, went to do it.

Joe [Califano] wanted time to find out what's involved here. And the groups didn't want him to have that time; they wanted him to sign it. Joe asked me to review it, to consult with people. Joe's theme was everybody ought to know what they have done here, the Congress ought to know what they have wrought, and we ought to advise everybody of what they are about to get hit with and ask their views about it, so no one can complain about the fact that this came as a surprise to them.

On February 17, after four weeks in office, Libassi and Arabella Martinez, the new HEW assistant secretary for human development, met with representatives of ACCD and other organizations concerned with the civil rights of disabled people. The meeting was the occasion for an announcement that Libassi and Martinez, whose responsibilities included the Rehabilitative Services Administration, would lead a task force to review the Section 504 regulation. The task force was to report within thirty days to Califano, who promised a decision "promptly thereafter." In a press release announcing the task force, Califano stated:

Although implementation of Section 504 has been delayed far too long, I have an obligation to the President, the Congress, and, most importantly, to our handicapped citizens to understand the regulations fully before I can proceed. I want to make certain that the regulations drafted by the previous Administration are the most effective way of carrying out the Congressional will in this area of vital national concern. I will direct the Department to focus on the proposed regulations as a matter of the highest priority.

Representatives of disability advocacy groups were disappointed with this delay, and publicly criticized Califano's plan for further review. They continued to press throughout the review process for immediate signature of the regulation as it had been drafted when Califano took office.

Libassi and Califano felt that it was unreasonable to be expected to endorse a regulation whose implications were great and whose legislative mandate was unclear. The disability advocates felt that they had been stalled for years by Mathews and that they were being stalled again by Califano. The result was tension, and the tension was exacerbated by Libassi's free-wheeling style, which treated no issue as settled:

It was a style which I felt most comfortable with and followed, which was open candid discussion with everyone about all the issues and what we were thinking about them. They didn't know how to cope with that. Because when I said, look, here's the problems that we are wrestling with, we want to know what you think, well they immediately went up the wall, because they didn't even want those issues examined. . . . When I said we want to look at the cost of what's involved with this, they refused. They didn't even want you to look at that issue. . . .Because of the style, which I did not change, I'm proud to say, saying here's where I'm thinking of screwing you, what will happen if we did that? How bad does it hurt and how does it adversely affect your interest? If you had to lose on four issues, you better tell me, because you're going to lose on some of them, and I don't want you to lose on something that's really important because I don't understand the importance of it. . . . That was very hard for them to take, because the Nixon people had never got into that. . . . That raised their anxieties. They said well what are you looking at, and I said we're looking at the whole thing. . . . Well that, my God, that threw them through the ceiling.

Califano directed the task force to prepare a report for him by March 22. Copies of the draft regulation were distributed to twenty-eight federal departments and agencies for their comments on its suitability as a model for government-wide regulations. Each of the major HEW agencies was asked to submit a plan for compliance with the proposed regulation. The task force also met with representatives of both disabled people and federal fund recipients. Major meetings were held on February 17, February 24, March 7–9, and March 23. Over forty-five organizations representing disabled people were involved, as well as a somewhat smaller number of recipients.

The Office for Civil Rights staff attempted to educate the HEW political leadership about the issues involved in the drafting of the regulations and generally urged that it be published without revisions, which might weaken its effect. Libassi described this lobbying:

> They were advocates. But they were not unmindful of the fact that the regs had to get out and so we had to shape the decision, and so they were very good about educating me as to what the issues were. I don't know how they felt, I always felt good about them. Oh, we used to argue and fuss, and we made a compromise. I'd want to change some things, and they'd say they were good. If they had rolled over and played dead we would have made a lot of mistakes. And so I valued them, and I hope they had the sense that I valued strong staff who would tell me what they thought.

As Libassi and Califano learned more about the substantive issues involved, they continued to raise questions about several of them, but were generally supportive about the concept of program accessibility and the overall thrust of the regulation. One concern was to avoid the kind of trivial but embarrassing provisions that undermine public support. Libassi explained:

> I was trying to make sure that we were not sticking stupid things in the regulations. I was more concerned about the obvious stupid things. Incidentally, while this was going on, to get my frame of mind, my first big decision [as general counsel] was to declare that boys' choirs did not violate Title IX. My second big decision during that period of time was that dress codes and length of hair should not constitute a violation [of Title IX]. . . . That was the kind of issue I was dealing with, which I think were stupid issues. . . . And whether girls were to wear pink graduation gowns and boys wear blue graduation gowns was a big issue I had to rule on. And that's nonsense. The federal government does not belong there. So while all this was going on, I was trying to be sure that under 504 we were really not being sucked into that kind of trivia, so that we could stand up and defend a responsible regulation.

The most vocal opposition to the regulation continued to come from representatives of higher education. Some OCR staff considered this opposition to be based upon a lack of understanding of the regulation and the concept of program accessibility. Libassi did not give the higher education representatives much credit:

> So you had some demagoging on this thing by the education people. The educators were very different in the seventies than they were in the sixties, and this affected education. The quality of leadership in higher education during the seventy-seven period was pretty dismal. Shameful. There was no leadership, no stature. I had some of my worst times with higher education people. I had one meeting where I just kind of lost my cool—I had been invited to

speak to some group, and I said you people ought to be ashamed of yourselves, all you're talking about is bullshit.

One issue seems to have been the subject of much interest by Libassi's superiors, the coverage of alcoholics and drug addicts. Both Califano and President Carter were opposed to their inclusion, holding similar reservations to those held by Secretary Mathews. Califano cites the issue in his book about his tenure as secretary, *Governing America*:

110

> It was the only part of the regulations in which President Carter expressed any interest. At the Cabinet meeting on March 21, 1977, Carter said he did not want drug addicts or alcoholics classified as handicapped. Carter had talked to Governor Jerry Brown, who had told him that a large proportion of the disabled in California were drug addicts and alcoholics, perhaps half of them in Los Angeles. Pat Harris [then secretary of Housing and Urban Development and later Califano's successor at HEW] volunteered her agreement.[16]

This issue presented a clear conflict between political and technical interpretations of Section 504. Virtually no one outside of OCR supported defining alcoholism and drug addiction as disabilities, because of their connotations of moral deviance if not (at least in the case of drug addicts) moral depravity. However, expert opinion was nearly unanimous in concluding that addiction to drugs or alcohol was either a physical disability, a mental disability, or both. In other legislation dealing with disability, both alcoholism and drug addiction were explicitly included. Thus the legal interpretation appeared to be fairly unambiguous.

Califano was uncomfortable, nevertheless, and sought additional guidance. He asked the attorney general, Griffin Bell, to rule on these groups' inclusion. He also solicited the opinion of a private attorney, Stephen

Pollock. Both sources provided the same legal advice—that alcoholics and drug addicts must be considered to be handicapped and therefore covered by the statute.

Continuing to seek outside legal advice, Califano asked Pollock to review the rest of the regulation. Pollock's initial report supported the previous work done by OCR, but identified twenty issues for further review. The task force also analyzed at least fourteen possible changes in the Section 504 regulation. Substantive issues being considered by Libassi and Califano included waiver provisions, allowing more time for compliance, and weakening some access requirements.

Demonstrations by Advocates

By the end of March, the task force and Pollock had reported to Secretary Califano, but Califano had not made decisions on all of the issues in question, and the rewriting of the regulation had not been completed. While this extended review was taking place, disability advocates were becoming frustrated. They were aware of the contemplated changes in the regulation through their informal contacts and from a March 31 telephone conversation between Frank Bowe and Peter Libassi.

The coordinating group of disability advocates decided that a dramatic gesture was needed to obtain public support and further pressure Secretary Califano into signing the regulation. The ACCD board, meeting in Denver, called for the regulation to be issued by April 4 in the version prepared before Califano took office. If the regulation was not signed by the secretary, disabled people would stage nonviolent protests in each of the ten HEW regional offices around the country and in the headquarters building in Washington. The largest contingents were to be in Washington and in the San Francisco offices. It was hoped that the sight of demonstrators in wheelchairs and with seeing-eye dogs would evoke public sympathy and force Califano to act. Frank Bowe wrote a letter to President Carter, urging that the regulation be signed, reminding Carter of his campaign promise, and threatening "nation-wide political activities."

A meeting was arranged for April 4 between Secretary Califano, Peter Libassi and his task force, and representatives of several disability organizations. The night before the meeting was to take place, a group of demonstrators went to Califano's house, along with television reporters. In his book, *Governing America*, Califano describes how he was afraid that his golden retriever would bite one of the demonstrators, with the resultant headlines "Califano Dog Attacks Crippled Woman in Wheelchair." Libassi recalled that it was not atypical for Califano to react in that way: "Joe thought only in newspaper headline terms. He saw every issue as it is on the front page of the *Washington Post*." The following morning, several of the leaders of the handicapped community, including Frank Bowe, Dan Yohalem, Deborah Kaplan, and others, met to plan strategy. They decided to state their positions and walk out of the meeting. The press was invited to cover the event.

The April 4 meeting was held at 1:30 in the afternoon. Califano began the meeting by explaining that the delay in issuing the regulation was due to the time required for someone not familiar with the issues to understand the justification for the various provisions. Califano then praised the sit-ins planned for April 5, comparing them to Martin Luther King's activities in the 1960s and expressing the hope that they would improve public awareness and support for disability rights. The disabled advocates protested the delays in approval of the regulation and walked out, with the television cameras rolling.[17]

Secretary Califano felt that the posture of the disability advocates was unreasonable and inappropriate to
the times. Libassi recalled:

> I had the Secretary meet with the group of handicapped
> representatives and they walked out on him. Joe Califano
> did not take kindly to that. He had put himself out, had
> been willing to meet with them, they asked him two ques-
> tions and then got up and walked out, and they had the TV
> cameras there taking pictures of them walking out. OK,
> guerilla warfare was a little passe at that point. It was 1977,
> and that was not going to move people on policy.

113

The meeting had been held on a Monday. On Tuesday and Wednesday, the task force met with representatives of recipients, including health organizations,
educational organizations, and public officials. However, these meetings were upstaged by the actions of
the disability advocates, who held a press conference on
Tuesday morning announcing demonstrations and pre-
senting statements of support by Representatives Edward Koch and Patricia Schroeder, and on behalf of
Congressman Brademas and Senator Williams.[18] Mean-
while, three hundred disabled people staged a sit-in in
Califano's office in Washington, while demonstrations
were held in each of the ten HEW regional offices around
the country.

The demonstrators in Washington stayed in Califano's
office all day Tuesday and on into Wednesday morning.
Califano was publicly conciliatory and privately fuming.
Libassi remembered:

> They stayed in the HEW building, the Hubert Humphrey
> Building, overnight, and Joe was really upset about that,
> because he did not want to sort of say this was a reawak-
> ening of the sixties. [His attitude was] we're not going
> through this crap any more. It's bad politics. It's bad for the

country. It's bad for the causes to think that sit-in demonstrations were the way the government was going to make basic public policy.

Califano would not allow food in to the disabled demonstrators and would not allow anyone to enter or leave the building. Telephone communication was cut off. The demonstrators used deaf students from Gallaudet College in Washington to relay sign language messages in and out through the glass doors. A sympathetic HEW employee rolled a bag of apples he had bought for the demonstrators past the security guards.

To Libassi and Califano, the public image of what was happening was of primary concern. Libassi would not allow guards to evict the demonstrators and spent the night discussing the regulation with the disabled activists:

> We agreed that evicting the blind and the halt and the lame on TV was not quite what the Carter Administration needed in its first months in office. Although the GSA guards said that they had to be evicted. . . . I said no way. With the seeing-eye dogs too? What are you going to do with the electric wheelchairs? Can you get them in the paddywagons? You guys have to be kidding. All I need is that. And dropping somebody. So they finally abandoned all notions of that, and they agreed that the negotiated solution was the way.

By morning, it was apparent to the demonstrators that Califano would not sign the regulations, but that Libassi understood and was sympathetic to their views on the regulation. A final dispute occurred over whether the demonstrators were to be allowed food, which was settled when Califano grudgingly allowed each disabled person one doughnut and a cup of coffee. Finally, the demonstrators decided they had made their point and left on Wednesday morning, after twenty-eight hours in the building.

Most of the other demonstrations around the country were more limited in scope and did not involve overnight sit-ins. In San Francisco, however, the group led by Judy Heumann, then deputy director of Berkeley's Center for Independent Living, resolved to stay in the federal building until the regulation was signed. The San Francisco demonstrators were supported by a wide range of local groups. Local Safeway Stores donated food, which was prepared by the Black Panthers. The local health department donated matresses. Individuals ranging from the mayor of San Francisco to Angela Davis came to pledge their support. Congressmen George Miller and Phillip Burton held hearings in the San Francisco Federal Building. Local city councils and the California assembly passed resolutions of support. The demonstration in San Francisco lasted four weeks, until Secretary Califano signed the regulation in an undiluted form on April 28. After learning of his action, the demonstrators marched triumphantly out of the federal building.

Participants in both the Washington and the San Francisco demonstrations recalled that staff-level officials in the Office for Civil Rights were supportive of the demonstrations. Several staff members of both OCR and congressional committees were involved in planning for the sit-ins. During the demonstrations, most staff members did not directly participate, but they were able to provide information to advocates about what was happening within HEW on a number of occasions before and during the demonstrations.

Those who were involved with the regulation disagree as to whether the demonstrations had an effect. For the most part, individuals who were working in the Office of Civil Rights at the time believe that the demonstrations had a limited effect, not influencing the substance of the regulation but perhaps causing it to be published somewhat earlier than it would have been otherwise. John Wodatch, for example, said that, as Secretary Califano came to understand the regulation, he became an advocate.

However, participants in the demonstration believed that Califano wanted to weaken the regulation substantially. They believed that their actions elicited public support and prevented Califano from deleting a number of requirements. Judy Heumann stated: "I don't think the regulations would have been signed without the demonstrations, as they were. I am totally convinced of that. I mean the political pressure was really getting to be heavy. They had to sign those regulations."

Publishing the Final Regulation

As the demonstration in San Francisco continued, the task force continued to meet and revise the regulation for final publication. Representatives of the demonstrators met with task force members, continuing to press for publication of the January draft. Some issues were resolved, while others, like the coverage of alcoholics and drug addicts, continued to be discussed. Legal requirements were weighed against political consequences. A draft of the final regulation was prepared and submitted to Libassi by Dan Marcus of the Office of General Counsel. A meeting was held on April 12 with Secretary Califano, Libassi, Marcus, Wodatch and Beckman from OCR, and a number of other senior HEW officials to discuss the remaining questions about the regulation. According to the minutes of the meeting, Califano on several occasions urged that strong provisions be retained. The secretary also continually stressed the need for a simple and short regulation.

On April 16, another draft revision of the final regulation was submitted to Secretary Califano. The draft included few major changes from the January version. It was shorter and much less specific and permitted greater flexibility for recipients in complying with its provisions. The draft exempted recipients with fewer than fifteen employees from a number of notice and record-keeping requirements. The coverage of drug addicts and alcoholics was retained, as were the other major components of earlier versions of the regulation.

An explanatory preamble for the regulation was prepared and final decisions were made about enforcement procedures and technical assistance for recipients. On April 28, Secretary Califano called a press conference to announce the signing of the final regulation for Section 504, which he said would "open a new world of equal opportunity for more than 35 million handicapped Americans."[19] Califano cited the following highlights of the Section 504 regulation:

- All new facilities must be barrier-free.

- All programs and activities in existing facilities must be made accessible within sixty days, unless structural changes were necessary, in which case they must be made within three years.

- Employment must be made available to the handicapped, along with reasonable accommodations. Pre-employment physicals would be prohibited.

- All handicapped children must receive a free public education without being unnecessarily segregated, and efforts must be made to locate and identify such children.

- Colleges and universities must make reasonable modifications in academic requirements and provide auxiliary aides where necessary.

- Recipients of HEW funds must complete a self-evaluation within a year in consultation with handicapped individuals and organizations to review policies and practices.

The regulation was published in the *Federal Register* the next week, on May 4.[20] Reactions were mixed. The disability advocacy community generally praised the regulation, seeing it as a victory resulting largely from their efforts. The changes that had been feared by the advocates and that had led to the demonstrations had not been incorporated into the final version of the regulation. Peter Libassi described their reaction as "joy and ecstasy." Frank Bowe recalled: "It was so wonderful an event. . . . There was just a tremendous sense across the country among people with disabilities that Wow! An unbelievable period of acceleration. And I got telegrams, so many phone calls, letters, everything. So many people having meetings, champagne parties, things like that." Many recipients, on the other hand, criticized the regulation, particularly on grounds of cost. Several recipients provided extremely high cost estimates based on the incorrect assumption that all existing buildings had to be made accessible and then complained that they could not meet the cost of compliance. Several journalists echoed these criticisms.

Proponents of the regulation argued that predictions of high costs reflected a lack of creativity and flexibility and that program adaptation could be made at a relatively low expense. Peter Libassi recalled the debate:

> Some of the big trade associations in Washington wanted to make a big cause about it. Some pretty narrow-minded people began to, afterward, yell and scream about this thing in terms of cost and so on. And I must say that my brothers in the architect profession didn't help very much, because they always wanted to find the most expensive solution to every problem. You know the drinking fountains,

big problem, oh my God, we'll have to move every drinking fountain down you know. The architects are going to redesign every drinking fountain to move them all down, and I would say, all you have to do is put up paper cups, they'll get their own water. You don't have to move a drinking fountain. The architects kept coming up with goddamned expensive ways to solve every problem.

In response to these concerns OCR director David Tatel issued a statement that reiterated the standard of program rather than total accessibility and suggested the use of nonstructural changes. It stated:

> It has been difficult to get attention focused on program accessibility because some people seem to skim over the regulations and explanatory materials and start fretting about the widening of thousands of doors or installation of high and low water fountains in every facility at every conceivable point. A result of the misunderstanding is a rising exaggeration of the potential costs of making programs accessible.[21]

Ultimately, a cottage industry of consultants grew up to provide advice to recipients on how to renovate for accessibility at a reasonable cost. One of the most prominent was a private nonprofit organization called Mainstream, Inc., which issued a report based on a survey of thirty-four facilities that the average cost for providing accessibility was one cent per square foot, a figure quite low in light of the fact that the same facilities spent thirteen cents a square foot to clean and polish their floors.[22]

In addition to the question of cost, widespread concern was expressed over the alcoholic and drug addict issue, particularly as it related to employment and to public schools. The specter was raised in the press of drug addicts working in pharmacies and of schools being forced to condone drug abuse. HEW, in statements by the secretary and in publications by the new technical assistance unit, emphasized that only "qualified" handicapped people must be employed. It was stressed that no employer would be required to apply different standards about past work performance or about disruptive or dangerous behavior. The statements also emphasized that rules about performance or drug and alcohol use could be enforced by schools and employers, so long as they were equally applied to all students or employees.

It took nearly two years for the Section 504 regulation drafted by the Office for Civil Rights staff and submitted to Secretary Mathews in the summer of 1975 to be published in final form. The final regulation was essentially the same as the initial draft, but its issuance was delayed by time-consuming administrative review procedures and a change in presidential administrations. A greater source of delay was concern on the part of political officials about the magnitude of changes required by the regulation.

Such concern could easily have led to a decision to bury the regulation or seriously dilute its impact. This decision was never reached, however, and two related factors appear to have been involved. First, advocates within HEW, centered in the Office for Civil Rights, were able to convince their superiors of the legitimacy of civil rights protections for disabled people. Once that legitimacy was established, OCR advocates were able to persuade their superiors that the logical and legal basis for the regulation as it had been drafted was valid. Second, disability advocates outside of government used symbolic gestures to create political, media, and popular pressures on HEW decision-makers to approve the regulation as drafted. Advocates within the department used informal means in cooperation with those outside the department who acted more publicly. Together, they were able to influence government policy on Section 504.

Policy Dissemination 6

The model for federal policy on discrimination against disabled people was established in the HEW regulation issued by Secretary Califano on May 2, 1977. That regulation began to be implemented immediately in programs funded by the Department of Health, Education, and Welfare. Further, it became the starting point for other federal agencies and departments, each of which was mandated to develop a regulation implementing Section 504 for its own grant recipients.

The requirements of Section 504 were also shaped by legislative changes and judicial rulings in the years following the issuance of the HEW regulation. However, the basic concept of Section 504 as a civil rights provision requiring substantial accommodation to the needs of disabled people remained intact, even through the early years of the Reagan administration.

Developments in HEW

After publication of the final HEW regulation, follow-up activities began immediately. Executive Order 11914 required that HEW develop standards for Section 504 regulations to be issued by all federal departments and agencies, and work was begun on preparing these standards. The Office for Civil Rights continued to respond to complaints of discrimination, but complaint-processing and investigation was delegated from the central office in Washington to the ten OCR regional offices. A technical assistance unit was established in the Washington office to assist recipients with compliance and aid disabled people in understanding and claiming their rights under Section 504.

In addition to responding to complaints, OCR conducted compliance reviews to assess what recipients of federal funds were doing to meet the requirements of Section 504. Further, each recipient was asked to complete a form assuring OCR of its compliance. These enforcement activities were similar to those taken for Title VI of the Civil Rights Act and Title IX of the Education Amendments.

For the various operating agencies within HEW, the Section 504 regulation was implemented without great controversy. Most recipients providing health services and many providing welfare and social services were already serving disabled people and had to make few changes to comply with the new requirements. It is difficult to assess the overall impact of Section 504 on these programs, but there was not a significant volume of formal complaints about them, and there was little public debate.[1] Every indication is that business continued as usual for federally funded health and social service agencies. Disabled people continued to be accommodated, perhaps in greater numbers. New buildings may have been redesigned and existing ones made more accessible, but there was no apparent great new influx of disabled clients. However, while assurances of compliance were filed, there is no overall empirical measure available of program changes or increased program use by disabled people.

For elementary and secondary education agencies receiving HEW funds, the requirements of Section 504 essentially duplicated the much more specific mandate under the Education for All Handicapped Children Act. Thus, no actions appear to have been taken solely due to Section 504 in elementary and secondary education.

The higher education community, on the other hand,

had been a center of opposition to the proposed regulation, led by the American Council on Education. While
ACE and other associations representing colleges and
universities had been critical of the proposed Section
504 regulation, others supported broader involvement
by disabled people in institutions of higher education.
This support was centered in the American Association
for the Advancement of Science (AAAS). An umbrella
organization of numerous scientific societies, AAAS had   **123**
been attempting to expand opportunities for disabled
scientists since 1974. One AAAS staff member, Martha
Redden, had devoted most of her time since that year to
promoting increased accessibility for disabled individuals in scientific meetings and institutions, and these efforts intensified following publication of the final regulation. Concerned with the negative tone of comments by
ACE General Counsel Sheldon Steinbach and others,
Redden persuaded the head of AAAS, William Carey, to
write his counterpart of ACE, Roger Heyns, suggesting a
more constructive response to the Section 504 regulation.

Carey's letter, on its own, could hardly have been
expected to carry much weight, given the sincere fears
about the heavy financial burden and the intrusive nature of the Section 504 requirements. However, Redden
and a few others in the Washington higher education
community were able to work through the institutional
network of higher education to build support for some
accommodation to the federal rules. Redden and her associates had knowledge of and access to this network as
a result of previous work on issues affecting higher education and because of the prestige of AAAS.

One of Redden's associates was Cornelia Bailey, a
staff member at the College and University Personnel
Association, whose husband, Stephen K. Bailey, was a
highly respected member of the higher education community. Bailey obtained a $10,000 Ford Foundation grant
to study existing programs for disabled people within

higher education. Her study provided a baseline of data about what colleges and universities were already doing for disabled students and about the limitations of these existing programs.[2]

The lobbyists for a number of associations representing higher education were key figures in interpreting government policies affecting colleges and universities and in shaping responses to those policies. The associations represented groups such as personnel officers, physical plant administrators, and admissions officers. These representatives met together on a weekly basis to share information and coordinate activities. Redden was invited to speak to one of these meetings, and brought with her James Gashell of the National Federation of the Blind. Redden and Gashell argued that program accessibility, if implemented sensibly and creatively, would not necessarily be expensive or burdensome. They contended that informal arrangements for accessibility could often be worked out at a reasonable cost and that the key to such arrangements was the direct involvement of disabled people in program planning.

The new head of ACE, Jack Peltason, was receptive to Redden and Gashell's presentation and asked Redden to consult with ACE about Section 504. The consultations ultimately became formalized into a project sponsored by ACE and other higher education groups known as HEATH—Higher Education and the Handicapped. A proposal was prepared by Cornelia Bailey and her husband to have the different associations within higher education conduct their own technical assistance programs for their constituencies. This project was funded with $100,000 from the Kellogg Foundation and another $100,000 from the Office for Civil Rights.

Initial training was conducted by Redden, OCR's Ann Beckman, and Al deGraff, the disabled student services coordinator at Boston University. Each association sponsored its own set of activities. The Association of

Physical Plant Administrators (APPA) gave workshops attended by over six hundred people and received funding from the Exxon Foundation for a publication called "Creating an Accessible Campus." The American Association of College Recruitment and Admissions Officers (AACRAO) published a booklet on admissions and recruitment. The College and University Personnel Association ran workshops and trained over 150 technical assistance consultants, and the American Association for Higher Education (AAHE) created an information clearinghouse, which was subsequently operated by ACE. Coordinated by HEATH, these activities were supported by federal funds, by grants from corporations and foundations, and by higher education associations themselves.

125

The projects run under the auspices of HEATH represented an important change in position for the involved associations. Professional associations serve as lobbying groups for their constituencies, but they also exist to provide services to their memberships. HEATH enlisted these groups to deal with the problem of Section 504 compliance in ways that they were already set up to do and that they could do well. Led by Martha Redden, advocates were able to redefine what had been a political struggle over federal intrusion and regulation into an essentially technical problem of how to provide access to disabled students as inexpensively and nondisruptively as possible. This transformation took place as the result of work by a few well-placed advocates within higher education and with limited but strategically used funds. Despite growing acceptance of Section 504, many institutions continue to object strongly to the cost of compliance. For example, the University of Texas and a number of other universities have resisted paying for auxiliary aids such as interpreters and attendants for disabled students.[3] However, the actual cost figures for complying with Section 504 have not approached the figures presented by college administrators when the proposed regulation was first published in 1976.

Higher education was unique among groups of recipients in its development of an articulated and institutionalized system for technical assistance. Attempts to develop similar support systems for health and social welfare recipients were far less productive, perhaps because they did not work successfully through existing institutional infrastructures. OCR officials and the private consultants they retained often lacked ongoing relationships with established networks of organizations and frequently had to develop support systems for recipients from scratch. Further, knowledgeable and energetic advocates such as Martha Redden did not always appear to mobilize implementation efforts.

In the implementation of Section 504 within higher education, three key factors were present in the successful cooptation of the institutional structures. First was the presence of in-house advocates who, while they lacked the authority to dictate change, did have prestige within the higher education community. These advocates were able to present proposals in familiar language and avoid mistakes based on ignorance of the unique situation of higher education. Second, these advocates were able to define the task of compliance with Section 504 in technical rather than political terms. Like the OCR staff when preparing the HEW regulation, higher education advocates treated an activist civil rights definition as a given and went on from there without serious challenge. Finally, advocates used their knowledge of interorganizational networks, organizational missions, and standard operating procedures to incorporate compliance into the standard repertoire of recipient organizations. While college presidents were voicing opposition to the concept of accessibility to the disabled, advocates had involved institutional infrastructures, often with some degree of enthusiasm, in the concrete tasks of compliance. The various higher education associations were enlisted in the cause of disability rights.

The accomplishments of Redden and other advocates working in the HEATH project were comparable to what John Wodatch and Ann Beckman had achieved within HEW. Deliberately, persistently, and astutely, they used their familiarity with institutional realities to get others to accept an activist/civil rights definition of Section 504 and thus institutionalize that interpretation at a sub-political level.

Beyond HEW

Section 504 applies to all recipients of federal funds and therefore to all federal departments and agencies that provide any kind of federal assistance for programs or activities. Since the passage of the Rehabilitation Act, however, the responsibilities of federal agencies other than HEW had not been formally spelled out, although HEW was clearly intended to take a lead role among federal agencies. In a letter to Caspar Weinberger written in November 1973, immediately after enactment of the Rehabilitation Act, several senators from the Labor and Public Welfare Committee had stated that the secretary had the responsibility and authority to "secure Government-wide compliance with Section 504."[4]

In August 1974, the secretary of HEW had written to the director of the Office of Management and Budget, Roy Ash, informing him that a regulation for Section 504 was being prepared, and that a mechanism was required to "assure uniform approach and effective enforcement." Citing the section's legislative history and the letter from the senators, the secretary claimed a responsibility for coordination and recommended that the president issue an executive order for the implementation of Section 504 similar to Executive Order 11764, which implemented Title VI of the Civil Rights Act of 1964. An executive order was issued, but not until a year and a half later, when the draft HEW regulation was first published. On April 28, 1976, Gerald Ford signed Executive Order 11914, which directed that all federal agencies implement Section 504 according to standards to be developed by HEW.

On June 24, 1977, the proposed rules for the implementation of Executive Order 11914 were published in the *Federal Register*, with a thirty-day period allowed for public comments. Fifty comments were received and, for the most part, they reflected the fact that HEW was addressing a new audience—other federal agencies. Many comments reflected an understandable lack of experience with discrimination on the basis of handicaps and with the concepts used in the HEW regulation such as program accessibility. Additional concerns involved coordination with the requirements of the Department of Labor under Section 503 and of the Architectural and Transportation Barriers Compliance Board under the Architectural Barriers Act of 1968. Finally, the problem of the cost and difficulty of compliance was raised again, most particularly with respect to mass transit programs operated by the Department of Transportation and to the public housing programs operated by the Department of Housing and Urban Development.

The final version of the regulation for the executive order was approved by Secretary Califano on January 3, 1978, and published in the *Federal Register* on January 13. Federal departments and agencies were given ninety days to develop their own regulations which were to be at least as stringent as the HEW standards. The regulations were to be published for public comment and reviewed by the director of the HEW Office for Civil Rights before taking effect.

Most federal agencies were slow to comply with the HEW standards, and none met the ninety-day deadline.

By the beginning of 1980, two years after the standards for compliance with the executive order were published, only six agencies besides HEW had issued final rules for their recipients on Section 504—the Small Business Administration, the National Endowment for the Arts, ACTION, the Department of Transportation, the National Aeronautics and Space Administration, and the Legal Services Corporation.

Developing regulations for Section 504 did not involve major legal or substantive questions. For the most part, agencies adopted regulations that were similar to the HEW regulation. The slow pace of rulemaking seems to have been based on the low priority of Section 504, its irrelevance to major agency goals and objectives, and the lack of sanctions available to HEW to force rulemaking. The task of developing rules was not difficult, but there was nothing compelling agencies to add to the regulatory requirements placed on their recipients. This delay was prolonged with the elaborate procedures for regulatory review instituted by the Reagan administration.

In response to inaction by federal agencies that had not issued final regulations for Section 504, the Paralyzed Veterans of America filed suit to require that final regulations be published. On May 26, 1981, a federal district judge issued an injunction against the nine agencies without final rules, requiring them to notify recipients that they were subject to Section 504 and that the HEW rules were to be used for reference until the agency had developed a regulation of its own.[5]

As agencies developed proposed and final regulations, the rules were reviewed by HEW Office for Civil Rights staff. When HEW was divided into the Departments of Education (ED) and Health and Human Services (HHS), HHS took over this coordination role. However, on November 2, 1980, President Carter signed Executive Order 12240, which transferred lead agency responsibility for Section 504 to the Department of Justice, along with responsibility for coordinating enforcement of Titles VI and IX. This coordinating role for the Justice Department has continued under the Reagan administration.

For the most part, the political turmoil accompanying the HEW regulation was avoided by other federal agencies. Once the civil rights definition of the regulation had become institutionalized in the regulation and the executive order, a prolonged socialization process ensued whereby, department by department, government officials came to view Section 504 as a civil rights entitlement to be applied with a program accessibility standard. With the adoption of agency Section 504 regulations, a legal basis was established for administrative complaints and private lawsuits by handicapped individuals who believed they had been discriminated against. In the absence of empirical evidence on the effects of Section 504, however, it is unclear how much these policies actually affected the operation of government programs.

In developing regulations for Section 504, most agencies followed the precedents established by HEW. One exception was the regulation for the Community Services Administration (CSA). The successor agency to the Great Society's Office of Economic Opportunity, the Community Services Administration, operated a number of community action and anti-poverty programs. CSA's mission and ideology were strongly committed to the protection of minority rights, and, once the idea of Section 504 was understood, the provision received a good deal of support among CSA officials.

This support was not only the product of ideological tendencies within CSA but of forceful advocacy from within the agency. The CSA staff member responsible for the development of the Section 504 regulation was a young attorney named Jill Robinson, who had been an intern at the National Center for Law and the Handi-

capped while attending the University of Notre Dame
Law School. Robinson had been extensively involved in
commenting on the proposed HEW regulation, and had
been a participant in the 1977 sit-in at the HEW headquarters in Washington. She had a strong commitment
to the disability rights movement and personal ties to a
number of OCR officials and disability advocates.

Robinson was able to convince CSA officials to develop a Section 504 regulation that was stronger than
the one issued by HEW. The CSA regulation provided
for a phased-in standard of facility access rather than the
program accessibility standard adopted by HEW. That
is, all physical facilities of CSA recipients rather than
simply the programs being offered would have to be accessible. Accessibility for an entire facility would be less
disruptive for CSA recipients (which included Community Development Corporations, state Economic Opportunity Offices, and local Community Action Programs)
than for recipients of other agencies since CSA programs tended to rent rather than own their facilities and
thus had more flexibility in locating themselves.

Robinson also included provisions in the CSA regulation that required translation services for individuals
with communication disabilities, such as deafness or
blindness, services not specified in the HEW model. She
described the rulemaking process:

> It was much briefer than it was most everywhere else. I
> wrote a draft, called in a bunch of both grantees and dis-
> abled people to sit down in a room together, [had] three
> days' worth of meetings with different groups each day,
> discussed the substance of the draft, and got input from the
> grantees and the disabled people together. It was based on
> the model that HEW had used. It was very effective, be-
> cause the grantees would say, "Yeah but we can't do this be-
> cause of this," and the disabled people would say, "Oh no,
> you can do that this way." And it was really wonderful,
> [they] sat down together, fought, and discussed the issues.

Robinson's rule was reviewed by the CSA general counsel and by the directors of the various offices within the agency. Some had concerns that were addressed through minor adjustments in the draft, but the senior staff and CSA director approved the draft substantially as Robinson had written it.

The proposed rule was published and about sixty comments were received. It was then revised, with minor changes, including the addition of a subpart on communications barriers. At this point, bureaucratic delays occurred due to a changeover in top agency personnel. Getting the new director to approve the regulation took several months. The regulation was then sent to the Department of Justice and the Equal Employment Opportunity Commission, according to the executive order, which had just been signed by President Carter. Both agencies objected to the stronger standards, and the facility access standard was weakened to cover only new buildings. The individuals in the Justice Department who were setting federal standards for Section 504 were reluctant to deviate from the established HEW model. The HEW standard had essentially become institutionalized. Robinson's attempt to develop a CSA regulation that was significantly stronger than HEW's had failed.

The CSA regulation for Section 504 was finally published on the last day of the Carter administration. The next day, President Reagan took office and the regulation's implementation was frozen. The content of the regulation was to become a dead issue, since the CSA was abolished eight months later.[6]

Another exception took place in the case of mass transit. While Section 504 regulations in most agencies did not involve major policy, there was a storm of controversy over the regulation developed by the Department of Transportation (DOT) covering mass public transportation systems. Access to public transportation has been the single most important public issue in the implementation of Section 504, and along with the debate over P.L. 94-142, the most hotly debated disability rights policy. This debate began in 1976, when DOT first required local transit systems to extend services to disabled people, and reached its height with the publication of the proposed DOT Section 504 regulation in June 1978.

The standard in the DOT regulation for accessibility in mass transit mandated that all newly purchased buses must be accessible and that all modes of transportation within an urban system, including rail and subway systems, had to be accessible. The public transit industry, represented by the American Public Transit Association (APTA), adamantly opposed this standard and argued for allowing localities to develop alternative "paratransit" systems specifically for disabled people, including the use of taxi or "dial-a-ride" systems. Some local groups of the disabled supported the development of such systems, which potentially could provide door-to-door service and would be far less costly in the short run.[7]

133

The debate between proponents of total accessibility and paratransit systems continued into the 1980s. Defending the DOT standard, national disability groups claimed that only the same access to the transit as able-bodied people had was acceptable and "equal," and that alternative systems typically only permitted travel scheduled in advance and during limited hours. They argued that the short-term cost of making transit systems accessible would be offset in the long run by the advantage of having a single system rather than having to offer alternative services indefinitely.[8]

Published on May 31, 1979, the final DOT regulation for Section 504 reiterated the strong standard in the proposed regulation that had won the support of Carter's transportation secretary, Brock Adams, and of several top career officials within DOT.[9] Since DOT subsidizes virtually all capital expenditures in local mass transit systems, all local transit systems were federal fund recipients, and the department had great leverage in implementing the regulation's mandate.

Some transit systems, such as the one in Seattle, responded to the Section 504 regulation by developing outreach programs to attract disabled transit riders. Many more systems complied grudgingly and sought waivers from the regulation. A number of cities formally requested exemptions, under another DOT rule that allowed anyone to ask for an exemption from any department regulation. Under the Carter administration, all requests for exemption were denied. Following the 1980 election, however, the Reagan administration weakened the Section 504 standard to allow local options such as paratransit.

Shifting Mandates, 1978–80

During the early months of the Carter administration, a number of members of Congress expressed support for the proposed HEW regulation for Section 504 and urged Secretary Califano to sign the rule without weakening it. There was virtually no opposition to Section 504 expressed in Congress throughout the debate over the HEW regulation.

Congressional support continued into 1978, when the Rehabilitation Act was again amended. The 1978 amendments, included in the Rehabilitation, Comprehensive Services, and Developmental Disabilities Act of 1978 (P.L. 95-602), contained provisions that strengthened and further refined Section 504 to include the executive branch of the federal government. Thus discrimination on the basis of handicap was prohibited "under any program or activity conducted by any Executive agency or by the United States Postal Service" as well as in programs supported by federal funds.

The 1978 amendments also formally defined the procedural remedies available to victims of illegal discrimination by extending to Section 504 the remedies, procedures, and rights from Title VI of the Civil Rights Act of 1964. The employment remedies from Title VII of the 1964 act were also extended to Section 504, but with the condition that the courts could consider the reasonableness of the costs of accommodation and the availability of alternatives in fashioning remedies to discrimination. This qualification was consistent with assumptions already made in the HEW regulation.

Another provision in the 1978 amendments made explicit the circumstances under which alcoholics and drug abusers were to be protected by Section 504. The provision was adopted as the result of public and congressional concern about the inclusion of alcoholics and drug addicts in the regulatory definition of a handicapped individual. Once again, the change formalized in the statute the policy already stated in the HEW regulation. The inclusion of this amendment was an essentially symbolic response to public fears about the mandatory hiring of alcoholic school bus drivers or drug-addicted hospital pharmacy clerks. The new statutory definition stated that the term handicapped individual did not include:

> Any individual who is an alcoholic or drug abuser whose current use of alcoholics or drugs prevents such individual from performing the duties of the job in question or whose employment, by reason of such current alcohol or drug abuse, would constitute a direct threat to property or the safety of others.

After 1978, the expansion of disability rights through statute slowed and halted. Some national disability advocacy organizations focused their efforts on administrative issues such as encouraging federal agencies to establish Section 504 regulations based on the HEW guidelines. A great deal of lobbying was directed at the Department of Transportation, for example. Legislative advocacy was concerned with issues such as the placement of rehabilitation programs in the reorganized Department of Education and changes in the SSI program.

136   The only major civil rights legislative proposal in the 96th Congress was to amend Title VII of the Civil Rights Act of 1964 to prohibit discrimination generally in employment on the basis of handicap. This proposal, sponsored by Senator Cranston, received widespread support from disability advocates but was never seriously considered in Congress. The automatic support in Congress for the extension of rights to disabled people had begun to erode, as consciousness of cost implications and organized opposition by mass transit operators and other recipient groups mounted and fiscal conservatism in Congress grew.

In 1980, the congressional backlash against strong accessibility requirements became overt when Representative James Cleveland and Senator Edward Zorinsky each introduced legislation permitting localities to develop alternative transportation systems instead of making existing bus and rail systems accessible. Other members of Congress introduced similar measures. None of these changes became law, but attitudes had clearly changed. The emerging consensus on Capitol Hill, according to several lobbyists and observers, was that disabled people were deserving of federal support, but that their needs had to be balanced against the needs of other groups in light of limited public resources. The blank check of civil rights entitlement had finally come up against serious political and financial constraints.

Judicial interpretations have also begun to waver. Since the publication of the HEW final regulation for

Section 504, several court decisions have dealt with major issues in the regulation, the most important being *Southeastern Community College v. Davis*, which concerned a deaf woman, Frances B. Davis, who had applied for admission to a nurses' training program at Southeastern Community College in North Carolina.[10] When the college denied admission to Davis on the grounds that her disability would prevent her from participating in clinical training, Davis filed suit in U.S. District Court, claiming that she was being discriminated against on the basis of her hearing impairment. The district court ruled that she was not an "otherwise qualified handicapped individual" as defined by the statute. Davis appealed, and the Fourth Circuit Court of Appeals reversed the district court decision. The college appealed to the Supreme Court, which agreed to hear the case.

In a decision written by Justice Lewis F. Powell, Jr., the Supreme Court reversed the Court of Appeals, ruling that deafness was a legitimate reason for excluding Davis from the nurses' training program. The Court held that admitting a hearing-impaired person would have required either eliminating the essential clinical portion of the program or constant supervision by individual faculty and that such basic changes in academic program were not required by Section 504. The decision was a fairly narrow one and did not clearly apply outside of professional training programs with particular physical requirements nor outside of educational institutions. The decision was based on the language of the HEW regulation and did not invalidate it. However, several advocacy groups and the U.S. Department of Justice had filed amicus curiae briefs supporting Davis's appeal, and many in the disability community were concerned that the decision might be a first step toward weakening the requirements under Section 504. Their fears were borne out, for the Reagan administration was to use the decision as a rationale for attempts to limit the mandate of the statute.

The civil rights basis for the regulations developed by HEW and other federal agencies has remained essentially intact through 1983, but it has increasingly come under attack by political conservatives. No longer universally accepted, support for strong and broadly defined federal guarantees of accessibility has weakened. Since the 1980 election it has become politically expedient to weigh disability rights and the benefits of accessibility against the costs of compliance, yet Congress and the courts have upheld the fundamental mandate of participating under Section 504.

Access for disabled people has been institutionalized as a civil right. While the means of achieving accessibility is being debated, the basic concept that disabled people are entitled to full societal participation has been accepted by most individuals involved in policy-making. Furthermore, the concept has been incorporated into law and the policies and procedures of federally funded programs. While the more costly elements of the implementation of Section 504 are increasingly subject to political give and take, a return to the pre-1973 status quo is extremely unlikely.

138

Symbolic Victories: The Evolution of Section 504

The history of Section 504 relates a sequence of events quite different from those typically found in case studies of social reform. Where social movements develop in response to some problem, and these movements seek policy changes dealing with the problem. The success of a movement in achieving desired changes is often based on its ability to wield political power.[1] The shape of policy initiatives is typically formed through the negotiations of various interest groups and their political representatives.

The addition of Section 504 to the Rehabilitation Act of 1973, however, was not the result of the efforts of a social movement or of traditional interest group politics but rather the result of a spontaneous impulse by a group of Senate aides who had little experience with or knowledge about the problem of discrimination against disabled people. Seeing an opportunity in a fairly standard piece of legislation, these Senate staff members sought to promote disabled people's participation in employment and other activities by prohibiting discrimination on the basis of handicap in federally supported programs. Because of their strategic role in the legislative process, they were able to do so essentially on their own initiative.

It would not be correct, however, to say that the Senate staff were acting independently of structural constraints and historical forces. Access for disabled people was a concept already being promoted by local political efforts and in such legislative precursors as the Architectual Barriers Act of 1968. It was also an idea consonant with other efforts in the activist 93rd Congress to broaden the legal rights of previously excluded groups. The Labor and Public Welfare Committee staff do not appear to have been aware of precedents for establishing the rights of disabled people, but neither were they working in a vacuum. If Section 504 had appeared to be beyond the boundaries of the politically acceptable, it probably would not have been proposed in such an offhand manner. Perhaps it would not have been proposed at all; a previous proposal to extend coverage of the Civil Rights Act to disabled people had been rejected by members of the Judiciary Committee without serious debate.

What accounts for this difference in response between the Senate Labor and Public Welfare Committee and the Senate Judiciary Committee? Some factors that may be involved are the policy networks surrounding each committee, the dialect of symbols used by each, and their respective goals.

The liberal majority of the Judiciary Committee was concerned with preserving newly won protections for racial minorities and avoiding dilution of federal efforts upholding them. The Labor and Public Welfare Committee was probably no less committed to the rights of racial minorities, but their primary concern was reauthorization of the Rehabilitation Act and assisting disabled people. Despite this responsibility, the Labor and Public Welfare Committee had little experience with legislating disability issues. It was their counterparts on the House Education and Labor Committee who had such experience as well as close ties to the professional rehabilitation community.

Section 504 was thus the product of a group with relatively weak ties to either the civil rights or the rehabilitation establishment. This marginal position may have permitted them greater freedom to depart from the racial orthodoxy of the former and the service provision orthodoxy of the latter.[2] Section 504 was not an unprecedented statute, but it may have had enough disruptive potential to have been considered only by people without strong institutional relationships. The form such a statute might take, however, was by no means inevitable, since the Senate committee's lack of experience with disability issues did not provide an obvious institutionalized response to the isolation of disabled people.

Since one staff member did have experience with another anti-discrimination law, Title IX, the language of Title IX (and thus of Title VI) was rather arbitrarily adapted into the forty-three words comprising Section 504. The use of this language was felicitous, since it evoked powerful legal precedents and symbolic values of equality on behalf of disabled people. Thus access for disabled persons became linked to the legacy of the black civil rights movement, a legal and generally uncompromising commitment to guaranteeing access to publicly supported programs and activities.

Creating this association was not the result of negotiation between advocates for blacks and advocates for disabled persons, nor was it the product of some broadly based movement for social change. It was the result of actions taken by a small number of well-meaning individuals who were not altogether aware of what they were doing but who happened upon a formulation that symbolized values likely to produce change and minimize opposition.

Most American citizens and most public officials were committed to equal access and equal opportunity for black Americans by the early 1970s, although with substantial disagreement over the means for achieving these goals. This commitment to civil rights had been reinforced by federal court decisions. As the association between access for minorities and access for disabled people became firmly established in the minds of both advocates and the public, disabled people were to benefit from the previous efforts and political strength of the broader racial civil rights movement.

Once Section 504 was added to the Rehabilitation Act, it received scant attention in the ensuing debate over the act's provisions. This lack of scrutiny was not unusual. Lawmaking in Congress typically is not a process in which a large proportion of members participate. A few specialists translate their concerns into a legislative proposal and seek to build a coalition of support based on a combination of party and ideological commitments and parochial concerns. Working out the specifics of policy decisions is then frequently left up to congressional staff.

The vocational rehabilitation program had received strong bipartisan support throughout its history. Once an item is added to the authorizing legislation by the sponsors on the involved committee, the particulars of the addition are rarely questioned or examined in any detail. This pattern held true for Section 504, and the impulse to protect disabled people from discrimination became translated into law without any debate and for the most part without the knowledge of potential advocates or opponents.

Once Section 504 was enacted, its mandate was in itself no guarantee of institutional change. Many laws passed by Congress have little or no impact in the absence of stipulated enforcement mechanisms and administrative support. But while Section 504 had no provisions for its own enforcement, because of its inclusion in the Rehabilitation Act responsibility for it was assumed by the Department of Health, Education, and Welfare, and HEW did not treat Section 504 as a routine rehabilitation provision. This turned out to be crucial to Section 504's evolution as a civil rights statute. Within

142

RSA, the primary federal rehabilitation agency, the underlying programmatic approach was to provide benefits and counseling to disabled people while enlisting the voluntary support of employers. If Section 504 had been assigned to RSA, it most likely would have been interpreted into an incremental and essentially educational program stressing voluntary cooperation. The Rehabilitative Services Administration did not want responsibility for the section, however, because it did not fit into the agency's existing activities. Section 504 also might have been assigned to some component of HEW where it would have been simply shunted aside as irrelevant to the prevailing agency mission and never seriously implemented at all. Such a response to the section seems to have occurred subsequently in several other federal agencies who had not issued their own regulations for Section 504 five years after the final HEW regulation was published in 1977. However, Section 504 was assigned to the Office for Civil Rights, whose personnel and ideology in 1974 meant that the section was taken far more seriously.

Just as the Senate committee staff's inexperience with disability led them to take an innovative approach to disability policy, the OCR staff's inexperience meant they were unlikely to respond to Section 504 in institutionalized terms as just another benefit or educational program for disabled people. OCR already administered Title VI and Title IX for the department, and Section 504's language paralleled these earlier statutes. So the activist civil rights attorneys of OCR drafted a regulation for Section 504 that set a high standard of accessibility to services, a standard that would require considerable effort and expense from recipients of federal funds. The standard was based on the approach that OCR typically applied to policy problems in civil rights. OCR staff members such as John Wodatch, Ann Beckman, and Martin Gerry were dedicated to an active federal role in guaranteeing rights. They were interested in broadening the conception of civil rights. The OCR staff easily made the linkage between Section 504 and earlier civil rights legislation and had an established repertoire of responses to problems of discrimination. A number of OCR staff came to identify with and strongly support broad guarantees of access for disabled people.

144
Another important factor in Section 504 rulemaking at OCR was the complex of relationships developed with individuals and organizations outside of the agency. The civil rights attorneys responsible for defining issues involved in discrimination and proposing remedies generally had little knowledge of or experience with disability rights. In the absence of a specific legislative history, they could not rely on the written record to guide them. The staff of OCR were writing a regulation in an area that was virtually uncharted. Working relationships were established early in the rulemaking process with congressional staff in order to get some sense of what Congress had intended.

However, the congressional staff who drafted Section 504 were also inexperienced in disability rights issues. Seeking more insight into the problem of discrimination, John Wodatch and his staff sought information and guidance from virtually the only ones then knowledgeable about the nature of exclusion on the basis of handicap—advocates representing disabled people. Many of these advocates themselves had only begun to understand and articulate the nature of barriers faced by disabled people and the ways in which those barriers might be overcome through institutional solutions rather than individual determination and resourcefulness.

Initially contacting individuals and later organizations, OCR staff drew on the experience of disability advocates. Disability advocates, in turn, developed and sustained contacts with legislative aides and OCR staff. Thus, a network developed that was made up of individuals and organizations with interest and, gradually, expertise in disability rights. The network initially served as a channel for information and concepts, which flowed from individual to individual and organization to organization. As the rulemaking process continued, linkages among the various parts of this network expanded and became more complex. Funds flowed from HEW to a number of disability organizations to conduct research and training and to provide technical assistance to other disability groups.

To a lesser extent, individuals shifted affiliations among different parts of the network, while informal sharing of the tasks involved in advocacy and rulemaking was far more common. Many of the individuals linked to the network saw themselves as engaged in a common task—the establishment of a legal right to full social participation for disabled people. Allegiance to this goal became, in a number of instances, more important than the formal role dictated by occupying an organizational position. Outside advocates contributed to revisions of the draft regulation, while several OCR staff helped to plan demonstrations and pressure their superiors.

An advocacy-oriented staff was needed to write a strong regulation for Section 504, but it was not sufficient to ensure that the regulation would be adopted as government policy. Final approval was required from politically appointed officials, who had to weigh any commitment to disability rights against the cost and disruptive potential of implementing the proposed regulation. The secretaries of HEW, David Mathews and Joseph Califano, were responsible for balancing diverse programmatic and political concerns and were more likely to consider both potential costs and potential benefits than were OCR staff, who were professionally committed to disregarding the costs of ending discrimination.

However, by the time the drafted regulation was submitted for secretarial approval, it had been developed
very carefully and with a strong legal underpinning.
Neither Mathews nor Califano attempted to eliminate
the regulation, although both looked into possible revision of its more controversial provisions, such as defining drug addicts and alcoholics as disabled. Both secretaries expressed their discomfort with the regulation by
delaying its approval. For two years, the draft regulation
was restudied and re-evaluated, but the final regulation
of 1977 was not significantly different from the draft produced in the late spring of 1975.

Some of this delay may be explained by the requirements of the formal process through which comments
from the public and interested parties are solicited and
considered. Further, some time was needed by each of
the secretaries to learn about the nature of the substantive and legal issues involved in the regulation. Much of
the time involved, however, seems to have been the result of passive resistance by Secretary Mathews and to a
much lesser extent Secretary Califano to implementing a
regulation they feared would be both costly and controversial. In Mathews's case, he also believed the regulation would not be in the best interests of disabled people.

Staff from the Office for Civil Rights could not dis-
lodge the regulation from this bureaucratic stasis on
their own. However, the larger network of advocates
could act more politically, with the help of insiders at
OCR. By 1977, outside disability advocates had become
well attuned to the culture and functioning of HEW,
and they had access to information about what actions
were being contemplated. Advocates were able to work
through their own networks across the country to gener-
ate expressions of support for the proposed regulation
to HEW officials, members of Congress, and the national media. Pressure was thus put on HEW political
officials to proceed with rulemaking, while opposition

to the regulation was typically weak and not as well orchestrated or well informed. Traditional popular support for programs benefiting disabled people was joined with support for fair treatment for victims of discrimination. Access for disabled people had become a goal it was not expedient to oppose. Further, support for the principle of accessibility became equated with support for the proposed Section 504 regulation. It would have been politically difficult for Secretary Mathews or Secretary Califano to have weakened the proposed regulation substantially.

Publication of the final HEW regulation for Section 504 completed the process of its institutionalization. The regulation became official federal policy, with virtually no competing models. When other federal agencies developed their own regulations for Section 504, they almost invariably replicated the HEW regulation, as they were encouraged to do under Executive Order 11426.

For the period covered by this study, the only recourse for recalcitrant officials of other federal agencies was to emulate David Mathews, whose strategy had been to delay and hope for better days ahead. There were few instances of direct confrontation with the well-organized and knowledgeable disability rights advocates. While the long-term fate of the various regulations for Section 504 and of the disability rights movement remains unclear, the institutionalized mandate of accessibility and nondiscrimination has had important consequences for disabled Americans.

Interest Group Politics and Section 504

The history of Section 504 presents an interesting case study in social reform, but one that appears to be atypical. What can this history tell us about more general forces at work in social reform and social policy? The pluralist model of interest group politics discussed in Chapter 1 cannot be used to explain fully the emergence of Section 504 or the reasons for its evolution into a major civil rights law. Neither disability groups nor recipient groups participated in the adoption of Section 504 into the Rehabilitation Act, and for the most part these constituencies were not even aware of its existence at the time. This lack of involvement continued through most of the period preceding publication of the proposed regulation in the spring of 1976. There was little interest group involvement either in the decision to adopt a government-wide policy of nondiscrimination on the basis of handicap or in the process of formulating what this policy would include.[3]

148

Rather, the adoption and development of a nondiscrimination policy was carried out by individuals working at the subpolitical, or staff, level. The degree of influence exercised by these individuals, and by staff for the Senate Labor and Public Welfare Committee and the HEW Office for Civil Rights, and the lack of interest group involvement may reflect the low political visibility of Section 504, which meant that political officials and most outside lobbyists focused their attention elsewhere. If many recipients had been aware of Section 504's potential impact, they probably would have sought to influence the regulation much earlier than the formal public comment period.

The policy-making process for Section 504 was essentially an open one. No attempts were made to conceal the development of the regulation, and expressions of opposition or support channeled through political officials would undoubtedly have influenced policy decisions. Receptiveness to outside pressure probably would have been greatest early on in the development of the HEW regulation, when there was little in the way of precedent to guide policy-makers, and decisions had not yet become institutionalized.

However, during the embryonic and more vulnerable stage of policy development, virtually no outside interest groups sought to influence the content of the regulation. Section 504 was a statute outside the jurisdiction of the offices and agencies with which most recipients were likely to be concerned, and rulemaking took place during a period when there were many other issues occupying the policy environment of potentially affected parties. Recipients of federal funds were subject to an increasing number of requirements and restrictions in the 1970s and did not have the capacity to monitor the multiple sources of potentially relevant information emanating from the federal government. Similarly, many groups traditionally interested in disability issues tended to focus on established benefit programs rather than on an obscure and apparently unimportant provision that was the responsibility of an unfamiliar agency.

149

Thus, the issue of disability rights was not particularly visible within the federal government during the early 1970s. The lack of outside involvement and the lack of guiding precedents created a unique opportunity for innovation by newcomers to the disability field. Because of Section 504's low political profile, these individuals were permitted a large amount of discretion in defining problems and proposing solutions. The work they did served to structure the issues involved in disability rights. Through the winter of 1976, the shape of Section 504 was determined by processes internal to HEW.

Outside interest groups had the greatest influence on the development of the HEW regulation from the spring of 1976 to the spring of 1977, when both advocates and recipients attempted to influence the final form of the regulation. Recipients were generally unsuccessful in having their suggestions incorporated into the regulation, while disability advocates were able to mobilize support for an activist interpretation in the final regulation. In neither case was there effective use of the traditional political resources described by pluralists.

Publication of the final rule in May 1977 meant that an activist civil rights interpretation of Section 504 had been successfully institutionalized. In its institutionalized form, the HEW regulation was not affected to a great extent by the objections of representatives of higher education or other critics. Similarly, in the Department of Transportation, the Section 504 regulation was not seriously affected by the vociferous opposition from operators of local transit systems until the Reagan administration took office. It was to prove difficult significantly to change decisions that had already been made, or even to alter the terms of the policy debate, until there were quite drastic changes in the political environment following the 1980 presidential election.

After the 1980 election, opponents of fully accessible mass transit were able to force regulatory changes, and overall civil rights enforcement diminished. For the eight years following the initial drafting of Section 504, however, conventional interest group politics of the sort characterized within the pluralist model were not much in evidence.

In fact, the model of interest groups influencing policy decisions was in some respects reversed in the case of Section 504. Advocates for the disability rights movement did not apply political pressure that resulted in the passage of Section 504 and the development of strong regulations; instead the adoption and implementation of Section 504 contributed to the growth of advocacy organizations representing disabled people and helped to orient them toward civil rights issues. Section 504 became a focal point for organizing among disabled people and a good opportunity for establishing policy-oriented coalitions of the new generation of grassroots disability organizations.[4] It would be going too far to say that Section 504 created the disability rights movement of the 1970s, but the existence of Section 504 did strengthen existing national and local organizations and contributed to the development of new ones.

The social movement of disabled people became better organized and more broadly based as the result of federal civil rights activities. The American Coalition of Citizens with Disabilities, for example, was formed as an outgrowth of contacts made at meetings of the President's Committee on Employment of the Handicapped. ACCD hired staff and opened an office with funds from RSA and expanded with the receipt of a number of other federal contracts.

Even many established organizations with strong membership bases, such as those representing blind and deaf people, gained significantly from participation in activities related to Section 504. Contracts for training and technical assistance to local groups were received by a wide range of disability organizations. Formal and informal consultations with policy-makers helped to legitimate both disability organizations and many of their leaders. A number of advocacy centers, such as the National Center for Law and the Handicapped, were so dependent on federal monies that, when funds diminished after 1980, they were forced to close or seriously curtail their activities.

Thus the relationship between outside interest groups and the federal government was not a simple one of competition by outsiders to influence policy. The relationship among policy processes, group formation, and political conflict proved to be far more complex in the case of Section 504, and it is likely that such complexity is present in many policy contexts.

Historical Trends and Section 504

Another explanation of Section 504 would characterize it as a logical extension of a pattern of expanding entitlements and services provided by the federal government based on broadly held social and political values. However, Section 504 does not represent a simple extrapolation of past programs, for it alters certain of their underlying premises. In the case of previous programs benefiting disabled people, Section 504 is a major step away from assumptions of dependency and incapacity underlying much of the vocational rehabilitation program. As for the civil rights basis for Section 504, unlike its predecessors, Title VI and Title IX, its regulation rejects the assumption that equal treatment constitutes equal access.[5] Section 504 was more a creative fusion of concepts from prior rehabilitation and civil rights laws than it was an inevitable byproduct.

152

The historical trends approach also minimizes the role of advocacy by concentrating on the almost automatic expansion of government action without acknowledging that effective political action is often required to overcome bureaucratic conservatism and inertia. Without advocates within and outside of the bureaucracy, it is unlikely that Section 504 would have served as any kind of catalyst for institutional change.

However, any explanation of Section 504 must use historical trends as starting points. They may be seen as broad realms of possibility, from which actual events and individual and organizational actors emerge. It is unlikely that legislation like Section 504 would have been enacted prior to the late 1960s, no matter how skillful its proponents might have been. Nor is it conceivable that similar legislation would have been enacted in the early 1980s.

In the period leading up to 1972 and the creation of Section 504, several specific background forces were significant. The first was the development of the vocational rehabilitation program and particularly its expansion as an element of President Lyndon Johnson's Great Society. The VR program constituted a commitment by the federal government to maximize societal participation for

disabled individuals, albeit through a voluntaristic program. A goal of full involvement in community life was
established, and a federal role in achieving that goal was
made legitimate.

A second background factor was the black civil rights
movement. That movement had been successful in gar-
nering broad political support in the 1960s for public laws
guaranteeing equal access in a number of institutional
spheres, including education, public accommodations,
employment, voting, and housing. It provided models
through popular actions in support of equal rights,
statutory language protecting those rights, and administrative structures for implementing formal protections.

The black civil rights movement (and to a certain extent the anti-war and feminist movements) also provided a repertoire of symbols for communicating its
goals to political officials and the public. It had created
an audience, both within government and among the
general public, already sensitized to those symbols and,
for the most part, supportive of the goals they represented. Previous support for disabled people had been
based on an assumption of dependency that was popu-
larly deemed to be acceptable. Such past support became coupled with new constituencies who identified
with goals of equal opportunity and fair play to be encouraged by laws guaranteeing equal access.

A third important background factor in the development of Section 504 was the expanding case law involving the rights of disabled people. While this legal trend
did not play a direct role in the initial drafting of the statute, it did provide a philosophical and conceptual basis
for much of the regulation and for subsequent litigation
involving Section 504 and disability rights.

Finally, the emergence of Section 504 as an important
civil rights law was fostered by short-term cultural and
political trends within the federal government during
the presidencies of Richard Nixon and Gerald Ford. The

widespread congressional dislike and distrust for the motives of Nixon-Ford administration officials contributed to a willingness to pass far-reaching and often unprecedented laws without much concern about their implications or about the problems of implementation. Such a stance on the part of members of Congress and their staff was shared by many liberally oriented professional staff in executive agencies, including the Office for Civil Rights. Accordingly, there were few qualifications of the broad prohibitions of discrimination in the statute and the regulation. Concern with the problems of administering Section 504 or with the consequences of compliance for recipients was not thought to be legitimate by those developing policy. The motives of critics were often considered suspect.

Thus Section 504 can be seen as the product of preceding historical trends and of its political context. But such a characterization by itself would not be adequate, for a number of organizational and situational factors were crucial as well. Understanding how Section 504 was related to its historical context is important, but is not enough to explain the distinct nature of its development.

Ideology, Networks, and Implementation

One important reason that Section 504 became a distinctive protection of the rights of disabled people was that it was not assigned to the bureaucratic unit previously responsible for disability issues. In the germinal stage of rulemaking, the primary consideration was developing an effective regulation rather than fitting Section 504 into the existing structure for the provision of rehabilitative services. The fact that much of the work on Section 504 was carried out by individuals without prior involvement with disability issues was an impor-

tant factor in the evolution of an essentially new regulatory approach to the problem of access.

The nature of the regulation was significantly affected
by the relationship between OCR staff and disability advocates. Because of the ideological tendencies within
the Office for Civil Rights, OCR staff were more inclined
to consult with beneficiaries of federal programs than
with recipients of federal funds in preparing the regulation. This situation was different from many instances of
regulation but was not unusual for the wave of regulatory efforts in the mid-1970s.[6]

The content of the regulation was largely a product of
the mix of participants involved in the issue of disability
rights, in what Hugh Heclo has referred to as the issue
network.[7] This network expanded and became more
diverse as rulemaking proceeded, but with expansion
changes became more difficult to negotiate and therefore were less likely to occur.

Growth of the issue network ran parallel to (but was
not the same process as) the institutionalization of the
regulation. As formal steps in rulemaking proceeded,
the effects of past decisions made changes more difficult
to accomplish, even when the individuals seeking possible changes had formal decision-making authority.

The thorough and fastidious work of John Wodatch
and his associates in drafting the regulation also helped
to ensure its survival in the face of political opposition.
Wodatch's staff had taken care to involve a wide range of
participants in rulemaking once the basic regulation had
been drafted. Consultation with representatives of other
agencies within HEW strengthened the regulation by
avoiding damaging unanticipated consequences, helping to neutralize potential opposition from within the
department, and gaining cooperation from prominent
individuals involved in the various substantive fields affected by the regulation. Similar efforts made by advo-

cates within the higher education community yielded comparable benefits.

Further, OCR's strategy of working directly with beneficiary groups was able, in part, to counteract the recalcitrance of recipients to comply fully with the Section 504 regulation. Building on relationships that had already been established, OCR staff sought to use disability organizations and individual advocates to encourage **156** compliance. This "bottom-up" enforcement strategy was not totally effective in forcing recipient compliance, but it did serve to multiply the efforts of the small OCR staff.

Symbols as Political Resources

Understanding the importance of symbols can help to bridge the distance between organizational decisions and broader social forces.[8] The words we use to define problems or to evaluate potential solutions to those problems structure thinking by linking concrete situations to moral categories. For example, whether an individual is described as crippled or disabled, or as a girl or a woman, may condition our treatment of that person. Architectural barriers may be referred to as inconvenient or as discriminatory. The former connotes a minor irritation to be disregarded; the latter a moral transgression demanding remedial action. Section 504 transformed federal disability policy by conceptualizing access for disabled people as a civil right rather than as a welfare benefit. By providing this particular symbolic context for the problem of inaccessibility, a new policy direction became established and ultimately institutionalized.

Shifting cultural values and changing power structures become embodied through symbols into organizational activities and specific policy decisions. Symbols help decision-makers deal with policy options by relat-

ing choice to larger categories, policy priorities, and social and political goals. Decisions, which may be con-
strued in a number of different ways, are guided by a
symbolic context that reflects some combination of ideological positions, political considerations, organizational
needs, and practical constraints.

Symbols may also serve as a crucial centripetal force
within the dispersed array of governmental and quasi-
governmental agencies, bureaus, commissions, and contractors. As lines of political bureaucratic authority become attenuated, symbols can be used to bind a wide
range of policy actors in pursuit of common objectives,
and to provide a common vocabulary for defining
problems.[9]

By linking particular decisions to broader goals, symbols help to provide a guide to choice. While many organizational decisions are made on fairly clearcut substantive grounds, many are also made on the basis of
symbolic associations. Decision-makers are particularly
dependent on symbols as a guide to choice as issues
become more complex and as agendas become over-
loaded. Most elected or politically appointed officials are
generalists with limited expertise, yet they are called on
to set policy on a wide range of difficult issues. To some
degree, they can rely on the expertise of their staffs, of
outside "experts," or of ideologically compatible interest
groups. However, these resources often are not satisfactory. Staff may have organizational or political biases
that shape their judgments and may also know little
more than their bosses. The policy world is populated
by experts with varying and frequently opposing views,
and choosing whom to believe may pose the same problems as choosing what to believe. And, in a surprising number of decisions, powerful established interest
groups may not be involved or may not be obvious.

Furthermore, government officials often must make
an enormous volume of decisions in a limited amount of

time. Thorough study and consideration can be precluded for all but the most important issues. Steven Kelman has observed this problem of overload in the Office of the President:

> The most important barrier to White House influence over agency decision making is the fact that time is finite. Although the capacity of the president himself and of the "institutionalized presidency" (the White House Staff and the Office of Management and Budget) to work endless hours is legendary, it is far outstripped by the stupendous number of important issues with which the agencies deal. The size of the institutionalized presidency keeps growing, but the tasks for government grow even faster, and they continue to overwhelm the president's aides. . . . Lack of time also means that intervention, when and if it comes, tends to come late in a drawn-out decision-making process and to be based on fragments of information rather than lengthy consideration that agency officials have given the question. It is "crisis-oriented." Thus it is often poorly timed and poorly justified.[10]

The constraints on rational decision-making have been an important theme in organization theory for at least twenty-five years. A classic statement of the limits on rationality is provided by James March and Herbert Simon, who suggested that decision-makers typically seek satisfactory rather than optimal solutions to problems.[11] The problem of making decisions in the context of limited time and information has been subsequently explored by March and his associates, who have paid increasing attention to symbolic influences on decisions carried out in ambiguous situations.[12] Faced with inconclusive or inadequate substantive guidance, public officials must make choices on largely symbolic grounds, and their decisions may be evaluated on symbolic rather than purely substantive grounds.

Through 1976, staff in Congress and HEW responded to Section 504 in fairly routine ways. Decisions were not simply a matter of standard operating procedures, however, nor of purely substantive consideration. Some decisions may be more fully understood as responses to the symbolic associations of Section 504. Discrimination against disabled people was to be unconditionally eliminated regardless of the cost or difficulty because civil rights were violated by exclusion.

In OCR, the symbolic meaning of Section 504 was refined and used as the basis for interpreting the section as a strong civil rights law. The consequences included disregard of cost factors, strong identification with disabled beneficiaries, and a prescriptive rather than an educational emphasis. Because of the absence of precedents and the lack of involvement by strong outside interest groups, the transformation of symbol into bureaucratically enforced regulation took place without serious debate.

Symbolic contexts are not inherent to any given policy problem, but rather are socially constructed, sometimes inadvertently and sometimes deliberately. It is possible to use symbols skillfully in entrepreneurial ways to frame issues and consequently policy decisions and policy outcomes. Crises may be defined into existence by prominently placed groups and individuals, including political leaders, policy intellectuals, media analysts, private corporations, and private foundations. Health care crises, fiscal crises, productivity crises, security crises—each of these became policy fads by translating long-term trends and chronic problems into crisis terms, often when manipulated by those seeking to create institutional change (and not infrequently to enhance organizational resources or individual careers).[13] John Kennedy declared a missile gap, medical reformers a health care crisis, police chiefs a crime wave.

Often an event is used to dramatize and focus an issue when actors define what is happening in ways that favor the solutions being proposed. The Soviet launching of Sputnik provoked a wave of school reforms. Thalidomide scares have been used to justify drug laws whose effects would have little relevance in the prevention of similar problems.[14]

Thus social problems can be "invented" and "marketed" by ideological and social entrepreneurs through the use of strategically expressed, ideology-laden symbols. Such symbols may be used independently of what we normally think of as power and can be a distinct form of power themselves. By invoking societal values, symbols can be used to manipulate or bypass traditional bureaucratic structures and processes. When a crisis is perceived, extraordinary measures can be justified and procedural safeguards ignored. A multitude of sins have been justified by the quasi-religious invocation of "national security," for example.

Individuals adept in using symbols to achieve political or social ends might be called symbolic entrepreneurs. By judiciously combining the use of symbols with other political resources, such entrepreneurs may be able to magnify their own power. The entrepreneurial use of symbols is clearly not the most important type of political power, but it can be a highly effective one. Symbolic entrepreneurship may often accompany other forms of political influence in a legitimating role. In some instances, however, symbolic entrepreneurship can serve as a crucial source of institutional change.

For example, the title of a bill may be more important than its substance in securing passage. Harold Seidman makes this point in citing the renaming of the National Microbiological Institute, which had experienced perpetual difficulty in obtaining funding from Congress because "no-one ever died of microbiology."[15] A new name, the National Institute of Allergy and Infectious

Diseases, was chosen to elicit more empathy and accompanying financial support. The change had its intended effect.

Symbols play a significant role within any organization or network of organizations. However, they are particularly important within the federal government. Members of Congress and many top officials in federal agencies must maintain a positive image among their constituencies, yet much of the work they do is complex and not very clear to even the knowledgeable lay person. Further, most governmental decisions involve a range of options, and what is done about any single option may only be understood in light of the alternatives. Frequently, the only way most office-holders can communicate with their constituents is in symbolic terms. The importance of symbols in national politics has been noted by analysts such as Murry Edelman, Joseph Gusfeld, and Thurman Arnold.[16]

The strength of the disability rights movements was based on the symbols it used to evoke popular support and support within the federal government. In the period between 1976 and 1980, disability advocates used symbols with a high degree of success in influencing policy on Section 504, both directly with government officials and indirectly through the media. Linking accessibility with civil rights meant that altering buildings and redesigning transit systems, at a considerable cost, was equated with providing for equal opportunity. Making job accommodations and auxiliary aids available were urged on the basis of fairness. Because of a civil rights definition, the costs of policy implementation were argued to be irrelevant to the policy being developed. This argument was also effective because the whole debate of Section 504 was shaped by the concept of disability as justifiable dependency that legitimated government support for disabled people.

The problem of discrimination faced by disabled

people was not defined in crisis terms, yet it was presented in dramatic fashion by disabled activists. The National Federation of the Blind has used blind people with white canes on picket lines to obtain media coverage and public support. When Eunice Fiorito threatened to surround the 1976 Republican National Convention with blind and wheelchair-bound demonstrators, she was able to persuade Secretary Mathews to publish the drafted regulation for Section 504. In general, disability rights advocates were able to build on public sympathy for disabling conditions and combine it with support for their goals of equal participation and self-sufficiency. Opponents were characterized as favoring welfare dependency and exclusion of disabled people from public life.

Just as economic entrepreneurs combine the factors of production in creative ways and then market what they produce, so advocates combined and marketed the symbols of disability rights in ways that gained a wide spectrum of support. Specific regulatory requirements for access and accommodation became attached to the symbols that were used to "sell" the regulation to members of Congress, HEW officials, the media, and the public. Without real political power, disability rights advocates were able to push the federal government into formally creating broad civil rights entitlements for disabled people.

The success of the disability rights movement took place at a time when many other social movements made claims on government. Such movements included those working on behalf of blacks, women, homosexuals, Hispanic Americans, Native Americans, Asian Americans, and elderly people, as well as those working for environmental protection and consumer safety and those working against nuclear power and nuclear weapons. The 1970s was also a time of activism by conservative groups concerned with re-establishing traditional morality and family relationships. They sought to influence government policy on such issues as abortion, women's rights, gay rights, school prayer, and the teaching of evolution.

A number of these new movements focused considerable energies and funds on developing the capacity to influence public policy. Organizations were created whose major purpose was to raise funds for establishing and maintaining Washington offices in order to monitor and lobby the various entities comprising the federal government. Another major activity was involvement in class action and other legal cases whose resolution might shape public policy.

Many such groups did not maintain strong organizational or other formal ties to the people whose interests they sought to represent. Rather than serving as representatives, they served as advocates. Such advocates sought to participate in political processes without much in the way of strong and consistent political backing. Rather, they typically made an essentially moral claim to represent the "public interest." Despite the lack of organized political support, advocates often were listened to, and not infrequently they were able to influence legislative and administrative decision-making.

As in the case of the disability rights movement, the power of many advocacy groups of the 1970s was based on sympathetic public officials who responded to the symbols linked with policy proposals. The pertinence of symbols was often increased by sporadic media coverage that focused on dramatic gestures and tended to translate complex issues into simple ideologically loaded formulas.

Successful advocacy, however, combined other political resources with the clever use of symbols. Many groups developed the capacity for good legal work and were able to win favorable court decisions that created or changed policy. Advocates also became knowledgeable about the policy process and were able to use this knowledge for strategic interventions. Finally, advocates sought to develop contacts and win allies within the policy-making and policy implementation bureaucracies. Such allies could serve as sources of information and as advocates themselves within government. The disability rights movement may be seen as a model of successful advocacy in the 1970s.

164

A power base built on symbols rather than mass support, however, can be unreliable and is typically transient. The receptivity of public officials or of the general public can change as the political climate shifts or because other issues command greater priority. Without more substantial and long-term sources of political support, the effectiveness of advocates can fade as new and different symbols become tools of political influence.

The Politics of Disability

The effectiveness of the disability rights movement appears to have peaked in 1978. Disability advocates were unable to obtain support in Congress for extending Title VII of the Civil Rights Act to prohibit discrimination on the basis of handicap in all employment, an important step beyond Section 504. There were few significant legislative advances after 1978.

Nevertheless, Section 504's implementation proceeded and a growing number of disabled people sought legal and administrative relief from discrimination. Disabled individuals were gradually becoming more visible in public life. A White House Conference on Handicapped Individuals was convened and a National Institute of Handicapped Research was founded. Whether these developments will have long-term payoffs that will offset decreasing political power is unclear, but disabled people are participating more fully in public life.

Since the 1980 presidential election, the decline in influence has continued and quickened. People sympathetic to disability rights have been removed from a number of administrative and advisory positions in federal agencies. Advocates have been unable to block attempts to weaken substantially the requirements for accessibility of mass transit systems under Section 504. Some of this apparent decline in effectiveness may be explained by natural developmental tendencies. Most movements have experienced the formation and dissolution of coalitions, personality disputes, and disagreements over priorities and strategies. Unlike some other movements, the disability rights movement has no single charismatic figure who serves to unify its various components and factions. To a certain extent, decline can become self-reinforcing, for in the absence of political advances the incentives for collective action diminish.

Furthermore, the decline of the movement should not be overstated. The disability organizations with strong grassroots bases have continued to provide membership services and to represent their constituencies. Most disability organizations have survived, but those that took advantage of generous federal funds to hire staff and develop programs have had to cut back seriously. In this respect, disability organizations have had experiences similar to those of many other advocacy and human service organizations with fiscal austerity and political conservation.

Much of the organizational apparatus of the disability rights movement has survived and probably will continue to survive. In the long run, the movement is very likely to achieve many of its goals. Removing many of the barriers to access is a one-shot task that has been widely (although certainly not universally) accomplished. Retrofitting transit systems or existing buildings can be very expensive, but accessible new facilities are not significantly more expensive to build than inaccessible ones, and barrier-free construction may become a routine practice.

Overcoming the attitudinal barriers facing disabled people will be a more difficult and necessarily slow process, yet it does appear to be taking place. Mainstreaming in public education is sensitizing new able-bodied generations to the nature of disabilities and providing many disabled children with the skills and confidence to become assertive and more fully participating adults. As both disabled and able-bodied people come to expect full participation without respect to disability, such participation may in fact spread. However, it may also be the case that only the most capable and motivated disabled individuals and those with less severe disabilities will gain acceptance. Those people with more serious disabilities, fewer skills, less motivation, or bad luck may continue to be excluded.

Whatever the success of individuals with disabilities in achieving wider social participation, the ability of disabled people to sustain a united and effective national political movement is unclear. In many localities, cross-disability advocacy groups have continued to form and in a number of cases to thrive. But at the national level since 1980, representatives of disabled people have not been able to wield their symbolic power as effectively as they did several years earlier. Their main efforts have been holding actions, urging Congress to limit funding cutbacks, forestall the weakening of regulatory requirements, and prevent the merging of disability programs with other human service programs.

While the future is uncertain, it does appear that disability rights advocates will have to develop new symbolic bases for their objectives if they are to be attained. The power of symbols, unlike the more traditional political resources, depends on the receptiveness of those in decision-making positions. There is little recourse for the advocate if those in authority do not respond favorably to the arguments of advocates. Representatives of the media, once an important tool in rallying public support for disability advocacy, have been much more critical of civil rights claims. Articles and broadcasts emphasize the high cost of total accessibility and question its desirability. The lever on the political system that still promises some success is the courts, whose reliance on precedent and greater distance from political concerns may provide a defense for previously established rights.

167

In one respect, the very symbols used by advocates have frustrated the achievement of some of their goals. Advocates have been generally successful in establishing the commonality between able-bodied and disabled individuals. The argument that disabled people should be allowed to achieve on the basis of their abilities, however, may have undercut the assumption of dependency that was the rationale for many disability programs. In recent years, disability advocates have demanded both equal rights and special services, and in doing so given the appearance of inconsistency. Different segments of the movement have emphasized different and sometimes conflicting goals. Some critics have used this apparent inconsistency in attempts to discredit Section 504 and other legislative gains of the 1970s. While programs for disabled people have traditionally had strong support among the public and in the federal government, it remains unclear whether this support can be sustained.

Whatever actions government takes, however, disabled people are likely to continue to seek greater integration into the American mainstream. This goal may be pursued legally and politically, but it will also be sought through the routines of everyday life. Here the future looks more promising. While attitudes and behaviors are more difficult to change than laws, they may slowly be yielding to the determined and widening efforts by disabled individuals to claim full social participation. Disabled people have begun a long march through the institutions of American life, and it is unlikely that they will easily be turned back.

Appendixes

AAAS	American Association for the Advancement of Science
ACB	American Council of the Blind
ACCD	American Coalition of Citizens with Disabilities
ACE	American Council on Education
AFB	American Foundation for the Blind
ANSI	American National Standards Institute
ATBCB	Architectural and Transportation Barriers Compliance Board
CDF	Children's Defense Fund
CIL	Center for Independent Living
CSA	Community Services Administration
CUPA	College and University Personnel Association
DAV	Disabled American Veterans
DIA	Disabled in Action
DOL	Department of Labor
DOT	Department of Transportation
ED	Department of Education
GAO	General Accounting Office
HEATH	Higher Education and the Handicapped
HEW	Department of Health, Education, and Welfare
HHS	Department of Health and Human Services

INSPIRE	Institute for Public Interest Representation
NACUBO	National Association of College and University Business Officers
NAD	National Association of the Deaf
NARC	National Association for Retarded Citizens
NCLH	National Center for Law and the Handicapped
NFB	National Federation of the Blind
NIPRM	notice of intent to publish proposed rules
NPRM	notice of proposed rulemaking
NRA	National Rehabilitation Association
OCR	Office for Civil Rights
OGC	Office of General Counsel
OVR	Office of Vocational Rehabilitation
PCEH	President's Committee on Employment of the Handicapped
PILCOP	Public Interest Law Center of Philadelphia
PVA	Paralyzed Veterans of America
RSA	Rehabilitative Services Administration
Section 504	Section 504 of the Rehabilitation Act of 1973
SRS	Social and Rehabilitative Services Administration
Title VI	Title VI of the Civil Rights Act of 1964
Title IX	Title IX of the Education Amendments of 1972
VA	Veterans Administration
VR	vocational rehabilitation

Appendix B
Research Methodology

The major source of data for this study was a series of personal interviews with participants and observers of the policy development process. Between July 1980 and September 1981, interviews were conducted with forty-three congressional staff members, federal agency officials, advocates, and representatives of nongovernmental organizations. Most of these interviews consisted of responses to open-ended questions and lasted between one and two hours. All but two of the interviews were conducted in person; the other two were done by telephone. Several respondents were interviewed two or more times.

Attempts were made to interview personally all the major participants in the enactment of Section 504 and the development of its regulation at the Department of Health, Education, and Welfare. Particular emphasis was placed on the period between 1972 and 1978. Several informants were contacted for preliminary interviews and asked to identify major actors involved with Section 504. Newspaper articles and public documents were also consulted to obtain the names of participants. In the course of each subsequent interview, respondents were asked who had been involved in key decisions and were also asked to suggest subjects for additional interviews. After several months of interviewing, few new names emerged. A similar "snowball" procedure was employed to identify influential participants in the policy development process from nongovernmental organizations and federal agencies besides HEW.

Interviews were obtained from all but a handful of the central figures involved. Important individuals who were not interviewed include Ann Beckman of OCR and Secretaries David Mathews and Joseph Califano. No interviews were refused outright. However, in several cases individuals could not be located or interviews could not be arranged due to schedule constraints. Broken appointments were not atypical, and it took several months to complete interviews with some individuals.

Most of the interviews were recorded on tape, from which verbatim transcripts were prepared. A few respondents preferred that their interviews not be recorded; in a few other instances, taping was not possible or the equipment malfunctioned. In all cases, extensive notes were taken during the interviews. All quotations given in the preceding chapters for which other references are not provided are taken directly from transcripts of taped interviews.

Interview data was supplemented by examination of documents and archival material. A number of published reports and documents by involved agencies, organizations, and individuals were reviewed. Press coverage of Section 504, related legislation, and the disability rights movement was examined, particularly articles in the *New York Times* and the *Washington Post*. Several participants in the enactment and implementation process made their personal files available to me, most notably Peter Libassi, Jill Robinson, Ann Rosewater, and Lisa Walker. I was also given access to the Section 504 files of the American Coalition for Citizens with Disabilities and and the Office for Civil Rights. Material from these files permitted me to reconstruct a number of poorly remembered events and processes from contemporary descriptions, as well as providing information on the changing positions and ideas of the various involved parties. Furthermore, these materials helped to counteract a major limitation of retrospective analysis through interviews—the reinterpretation of past motives, understandings, and events over time.

With the exception of one ex-congressional staff member who dismissed both my research and Section 504 as "bull," everyone contacted for this research was

172

cooperative. Most of those interviewed were enthusiastic about the prospect of a written history of the development of Section 504 and supported the purposes of the study. Although people's interpretations of events varied with their institutional and personal roles, a generally coherent picture of what happened and why emerged from the research.

APPENDIX C

List of Persons Interviewed and
Their Major Organizational Affiliations
During Period Studied

Chris Alvarez	Office of Senator Cranston
Kathaleen (Kay) Arneson	RSA
James Bennett	OCR, HEW; HHS
Frank Bowe	ACCD
Edward Carney	NAD
Martin Convesser	DOT
Jack Duncan	RSA; House Subcommittee on Select Education
Nik Edes	Senate Committee on Labor and Public Welfare; DOL
Eunice Fiorito	ACCD; RSA
Rebecca Fitch	NARC; OCR, HEW; HHS
Sally Foley	OCR, HEW; HHS
Patria Forsythe	Senate Subcommittee on the Handicapped
Michael Francis	Senate Committee on Labor and Public Welfare; Office of Senator Stafford
James Gashell	NFB
Martin Gerry	OCR, HEW
Charles Goldman	ATBCB

Carl Goodman	ATBCB
Betty Griffin	Senate Subcommittee on the Handicapped
R. Claire Guthrie	Princeton University; ACE
Rhona Hartmann	HEATH
Judy Heumann	DIA; Senate Labor and Public Welfare Committee; CIL; ACCD
Robert Humphreys	Senate Labor and Public Welfare Committee; RSA
Robin Jenkins	NACUBO
Raymond (Bud) Keith	OCR, HEW; OCR, HHS
John Lancaster	PVA; ACCD
Peter Libassi	HEW
Edward Lynch	OCR, HEW; OCR, ED
Durwood McDaniel	ACB
Peter Myette	ACCD
Bernard Posner	PCEH
Martha Redden	AAAS
Jill Robinson	NCLH; CSA
Reese Robrahn	ACB; ACCD
Ann Rosewater	CDF; Office of Congressman George Miller
Jonathan Steinberg	Senate Committee on Labor and Public Welfare
Richard Sternberg	OCR, ED
Ned Stuttman	PILCOP; OCR, ED
Judy Wagner	House Subcommittee on Select Education
Lisa Walker	Senate Subcommittee on Labor and Public Welfare
John Williams	ACCD
John Wodatch	OCR, HEW; OCR, ED; Justice Department

Appendix D
Summary of Major Findings from the
Inflation Impact Statement on the Costs of
Implementing Section 504 for HEW Programs

The following summary is taken from Dave M. O'Neill,
"Discrimination Against Handicapped Persons," *Federal
Register*, May 17, 1976, pp. 20312–80.

Employment

- For most jobs and most handicapping conditions,
  "reasonable accommodation" would require only minor expenditures, if any.

- The HEW regulation would affect approximately one
  million workers in state and local government and in
  private institutions receiving federal funds. The annual earnings of these workers might be reduced by
  as much as 18 percent because of employment discrimination. Based on these figures, disabled workers
  would earn approximately one billion dollars more if
  discrimination were eliminated.

- The major cost of reasonable accommodation would
  be making buildings physically accessible to disabled
  workers.

- Based on surveys by the Civil Service Commission,
  DuPont, and others of the costs of accommodating
  disabled employees, accommodations required of employers would not involve very much job restructur-
  ing or worksite modification, and the costs of such
  changes would be slight.

- There was no evidence to suggest that employing disabled workers would decrease safety performance or
  decrease disability and life insurance rates.

Program Accessibility

- The cost of barrier-free construction was estimated at 0.5 percent of the total cost of new construction. This low percentage increase, together with the existence of other federal and state requirements for accessibility, would render the economic impact of the program accessibility provision insignificant.

- The total estimated cost of altering enough existing facilities to meet the standard of program accessibility would be between $216 and $475 million, or an annualized cost of $50 million. This includes the cost of accessibility for elementary and secondary education, higher education, hospitals and nursing facilities, and welfare and rehabilitation service buildings.

- Benefits from accessibility would include reduced costs of providing education to some handicapped children, increased lifetime earning capacity of those handicapped individuals obtaining further education, and increased earnings capacity for handicapped workers having access to jobs in accessible buildings.

Elementary and Secondary Education

- Many of the costs of expanded special education services would be attributable to changes required by P.L. 94-142 as well as Section 504.

- A major source of cost increase would be the extension of some form of education and training to all severely and profoundly handicapped children. The cost was estimated at about $5,000 per year per child, with anywhere between 50,000 and 500,000 children affected.

- The other source of cost increase would be the extension of free services to all of the moderate and mildly handicapped children not now receiving services. With the addition of this group, the total cost increase was estimated at from $1.8 to $4.8 billion, depending upon the prevalence rates for such poorly defined conditions as learning disabilities, the age range of children to be covered, and differing cost assumptions.

- Offsetting cost decreases might result from the reduction of mislabeling and misassignment and the integration of physically handicapped children due to physical accessibility. Cost decrease estimates ranged from $450 to $805 million.

Higher Education

- The major cost for higher education institutions would be associated with attaining building accessibility. It was not anticipated that requirements for nondiscrimination in recruitment, admissions, and provision of courses and noncurricular services would impose significant additional costs.

- Even if costs were to rise perceptibly, they would be balanced by benefits from the increased earnings capacity of those additional disabled individuals who would earn college degrees. If the percentage of severely disabled graduating college were to increase from 3.3 percent to 6.0 percent, the annual flow of benefits would eventually rise to about $100 million.

- The cost of auxiliary aids would be borne in part by vocational rehabilitation agencies. Those borne by the higher education institutions should not be substantial if enforcement were done in a manner allowing flexibility in means of compliance.

Appendixes

Health and Social Services

- Because health and social service systems were already structured to permit the participation of handicapped clients, such systems should not bear substantial additional costs.

- Cost would be further limited by providing for the special needs of small providers of services.

Notes

Chapter 1

1. Many people with disabling conditions prefer to be called disabled rather than handicapped, claiming that "handicaps" are unnecessary social restrictions placed on them as a result of their disabilities. The term disabled will be used here, although the words handicapped and disabled are often used interchangeably in the literature.

2. U.S. Senate, *Senate Report 93-318*, 93rd Cong., 1st Sess. (Washington, D.C.: U.S. Government Printing Office, 1973), p. 70.

3. U.S. House of Representatives, *House Report 93-500*, 93rd Cong., 1st Sess. (Washington, D.C.: U.S. Government Printing Office, 1973), p. 41.

4. This discussion is based in large part on a personal communication from Janet Francendese.

5. President's Committee on Employment of the Handicapped, *One in Eleven: Handicapped Adults in America* (Washington, D.C.: U.S. Government Printing Office, 1977).

6. Developmental disabilities were defined in the statutes as including several categories of disability, including mental retardation, epilepsy, cerebral palsy, and autism. This definition was revised in 1978 to a functional definition based on long-term impairment in various activities.

7. Erving Goffman, *Stigma* (Englewood Cliffs: Prentice-Hall, 1963).

8. Frank Laski, "Legal Strategies to Secure Entitlement to Services for Severely Handicapped Persons," paper presented at Conference on Habilitation of Severely Handicapped Adults, Public Interest Law Center of Philadelphia, May 12, 1978, p. 1.

Notes

9. Among the classic statements of the pluralist perspective are Robert Dahl, *Who Governs?* (New Haven: Yale University Press, 1961); Edward Banfield, *Political Influence* (New York: Free Press, 1961); and David B. Truman, "Interest Groups and the Nature of the State," in *American Society, Inc.*, ed. Maurice Zeitlin (Chicago: Markham, 1970), pp. 317–38.

10. U.S. Bureau of Census, Report PC(2)-6C: *Persons with Work Disability* (Washington, D.C.: U.S. Government Printing Office, 1973).

11. Daniel Bell, *The Cultural Contradictions of Capitalism* (New York: Basic Books, 1976). This perspective is consistent with the perspective of functionalist sociology on social reform. See, for example, Talcott Parsons, "Full Citizenship for the Negro American: A Sociological Problem," *Daedalus* 94, no. 4 (Nov. 1965): 1009–54.

Chapter 2

1. Some of these early institutions for the disabled are discussed in Esco C. Oberman, "History and Philosophy," in *Madison Lectures on Vocational Rehabilitation*, ed. George N. Wright (Madison: Rehabilitation Counselor Education Program, University of Wisconsin, 1967).

2. The growth and transformation of institutions in nineteenth-century America is described in David J. Rothman, *The Discovery of the Asylum: Social Order and Disorder in the New Republic* (Boston: Little, Brown, 1971).

3. The development of vocational education programs in the Progressive Era is described in Lawrence A. Cremin, *The Transformation of the School: Progressivism in American Education, 1876–1957* (New York: Vintage, 1964). A more critical description is provided in Joel Spring, *Education and the Rise of the Corporate State* (Boston: Beacon, 1972).

4. The development of industrial psychology is described in Reinhard Bendix, *Work and Authority in Industry: Ideologies of Management in the Course of Industrialization* (Berkeley: University of California Press, 1974), and Harry Braver-

man, *Labor and Monopoly Capital: The Degradation of Work in the Twentieth Century* (New York: Monthly Review, 1974).

5.   The history of the vocational rehabilitation program is described in Wright, ed., *Madison Lectures on Vocational Rehabilitation*, and in John G. Cull and Richard E. Hardy, *Vocational Rehabilitation: Profession and Process* (Springfield, Ill.: Charles C. Thomas, 1972).

6.   For a full description of the act, see Bureau of National Affairs, *The Civil Rights Act of 1964* (Washington, D.C.: The Bureau, 1964).

7.   Two of the most important decisions were *Brown v. Board of Education* (347 U.S. 483 (1954)) and *Swann v. Charlotte–Mecklenburg Board of Education* (402 U.S. 1 (1971)).

8.   This role was to be subsequently weakened when Congress prohibited the cutoff of funds to school systems when busing was to be the means of desegregation.

9.   An analysis of the implementation of Title VI with regard to school desegregation is provided in Beryl A. Radin, *Implementation, Change, and the Federal Bureaucracy: School Desegregation Policy in HEW, 1964–1968* (New York: Teachers College Press, 1977), and in Gary Orfield, *The Reconstruction of Southern Education: The Schools and the 1964 Civil Rights Act* (New York: Wiley-Interscience, 1969).

10.   An examination of these laws and the social movement that produced them is given in Jo Freeman, *The Politics of Women's Liberation* (New York: Longman, 1975).

11.   The application of Title IX is also limited in that it exempts single-sex schools, private undergraduate colleges, and military academies from its requirements for nondiscriminatory admissions policies and procedures.

12.   One exception was a 1968 New York City ordinance that applied to any disabled person who used an aid or a device and thus included both those using white canes and orthopedically impaired people using wheelchairs, crutches, and other means of assistance. The law did not cover disabled people who did not use such aids, however, and, according to

a former director of the New York City Mayor's Office for the Handicapped, it was never seriously enforced.

13.   Personal interview with Kay Arneson. All quotations that follow that are not otherwise attributed are taken verbatim from personal interviews conducted by the author between July 1980 and September 1981.

14.   Enforcement mechanisms were added in the Rehabilitation Act of 1973 with the creation of the Architectural Barriers Compliance Board, and strengthened under the 1978 Rehabilitation Act Amendments, which renamed the enforcement body the Architectural and Transportation Barriers Compliance Board (ATBCB).

15.   The development of subcultures within institutions is described in Erving Goffman, *Asylums: Essays on the Social Situation of Mental Patients and Other Inmates* (Garden City, N.Y.: Anchor, 1961).

16.   Ibid., pp. 23–24.

17.   Ibid., pp. 24–31.

18.   John Lenihan, "Disabled Americans: A History," *Performance* 27, nos. 5–7 (Nov. 1976–Jan. 1977): 1–72.

19.   As neonatology and screening programs become more sophisticated, many disabling conditions should be prevented or controlled. It is likely that the profile of disabilities in the population will continue to change in the coming decades.

20.   Roberts later was appointed director of vocational rehabilitation for the State of California.

21.   Susan Bliss, "The Mobilization of DIA," *Performance* 22, nos. 11–12 (May–June 1972): 3–7.

22.   Similar legal rights centers had been established in the 1960s to work on behalf of poor people and minorities in the wake of the Great Society and the War on Poverty programs, some under the sponsorship of the federal Office of Economic Opportunity.

23.   325 F. Supp. 781 (M.D. Ala. 1971).

24. 324 F. Supp. 1257 (E.D. Pa. 1971).

25. 348 F. Supp. 866 (D.D.C. 1972).

26. Martin H. Gerry and J. Martin Benton, "Section 504: Expanding Educational Opportunities," unpublished paper, Oct. 31, 1980, p. 4.

27. Ibid., p. 3.

Chapter 3

1. S. 3094, 92nd Congress, 2nd session (1972).

2. H.R. 12154, 92nd Congress, 2nd session (1972).

3. U.S. Congress, *Congressional Record* (Washington, D.C.: U.S. Government Printing Office, Jan. 20, 1972), p. 526.

4. The Labor and Public Welfare Committee is now called the Labor and Human Resources Committee, a change in accordance with the general purging of the word welfare from government usage.

5. All otherwise unattributed quotations have been taken from verbatim transcripts of interviews conducted by the author.

6. The GAO report is summarized in Cornelia W. Bailey, *The Federal 504 Handicapped Access Regulations: A Case Study in Government–Higher Education Relations* (Cambridge, Mass.: Sloan Commission on Government and Higher Education, Jan. 31, 1979), p. 5.

7. An analysis of the role of staff in Congress is given in Michael J. Malbin, *Unelected Representatives* (New York: Basic Books, 1982).

8. Section 501 created the Interagency Committee on Handicapped Federal Employees and required each federal agency to develop and implement affirmative action programs for the hiring, placement, and advancement of handicapped employees. Section 502 created the Architectural and Transportation Barriers Compliance Board. The ATBCB was mandated to ensure compliance with the Architectural Barriers Act

Notes

of 1968, which required that all new federal buildings be accessible to disabled people and that all renovations provide for accessibility. It was given a budget of one million dollars a year and authorized to hire a staff and "issue such orders as it deems necessary to insure compliance" with the Barriers Act. Section 503 of the act required that all federal contracts in excess of $2,500 contain a provision requiring affirmative action in employment by the contractor. The provision was implemented and enforced by the Office of Federal Contract Compliance Programs in the Department of Labor.

9. Frank G. Bowe, *Handicapping America* (New York: Harper and Row, 1978), p. 205.

10. S. 7, 93rd Congress, 1st session (1973).

11. Hearings Before the Subcommittee on the Handicapped of the Committee on Labor and Public Welfare on S. 7, U.S. Senate, 93rd Congress, 1st session, Jan. 10, 1973, pp. 282–83.

12. See, for example, Jeremy Rabkin, "Office for Civil Rights," in *The Politics of Regulation*, ed. James Q. Wilson (New York: Basic Books, 1980), pp. 304–53.

Chapter 4

1. Congress frequently enacts legislation stating policy goals that may never be achieved, such as full employment or universally available affordable housing.

2. There were several provisions in the Rehabilitation Act that Congress had delegated outside of HEW. Implementation of Section 503, for example, was the responsibility of the Department of Labor's Office of Federal Contract Compliance Programs.

3. Letter from Senate Subcommittee on the Handicapped to HEW Secretary Caspar Weinberger, Nov. 13, 1973.

4. Personal interview with Martin Gerry.

5. Wilson notes the tendency for attorneys to approach conflict resolution in adversarial proceedings conducted by advocates (James Q. Wilson, "The Politics of Regulation," in

The Politics of Regulation, ed. James Q. Wilson [New York: Basic Books, 1980], p. 380).

6. The ideology of HEW civil rights attorneys in the 1960s is described in Beryl A. Radin, *Implementation, Change, and the Federal Bureaucracy: School Desegregation Policy in HEW, 1964–1968* (New York: Teachers College Press, 1977), pp. 129–31.

7. Jeremy Rabkin, "Office for Civil Rights," in *Politics of Regulation*, ed. Wilson, pp. 304–53.

8. 414 U.S. 564.

9. H.R. 17503, 93rd Congress, 2nd session (1974).

10. U.S. Senate, *Senate Report 93-1297*, 93rd Congress, 2nd session (Washington, D.C.: U.S. Government Printing Office, 1974).

11. Shortly after receiving responsibility for the section, the Office for Civil Rights had asked the Office of General Counsel for an opinion as to whether they had authority to proceed with regulations. The attorneys in that office found that the statute was "mandatory" and that it therefore required an implementing regulation. Nevertheless, the department was on much safer ground after its authority to proceed was ratified by Congress in the conference report.

12. Memorandum from John Wodatch to Peter Holmes, Jan. 18, 1975.

13. Similar conceptual problems are involved in legal prohibitions of discrimination based on age. These problems are addressed in Peter H. Schuck, "The Graying of Civil Rights Law: The Age Discrimination Act of 1975," *Yale Law Journal* 89 (1979): 27–93.

14. Memorandum from John Wodatch to Peter Holmes, Feb. 20, 1975.

15. The ANSI standards were revised in 1975 at Syracuse University under the sponsorship of PCEH, the Department of Housing and Urban Development, and the National Easter Seal Society.

16. "Programs and Activities Receiving or Benefiting From Federal Financial Assistance: Nondiscrimination on the basis of Handicap," *Federal Register*, July 16, 1976, p. 29550.

17. Several years later, the unique cost problems involved in providing access to disabled people were recognized by Gerry: "I must say that that issue, that cost issue, is something I misjudged. Misjudged the potency of it and I think I didn't fully understand. I guess part of it was simply the lack of understanding of what a lot of these things were and how much they cost. . . . You have to have staff that understand the programs of the other agencies sufficiently well to do that."

18. A similar benefit/cost analysis is made in Frank G. Bowe, *Handicapping America* (New York: Harper and Row, 1978). Such analyses of programs for disabled people are discussed in Sar A. Levitan and Robert Taggert, *Jobs for the Disabled* (Baltimore: Johns Hopkins University Press, 1977).

19. Steven Kelman has observed a similar deliberate disregard for cost factors in another federal regulatory agency, the Occupational Safety and Health Administration (OSHA). He suggests that governmental employees may have a stronger ideological commitment to "nonmaterial" considerations, and that they may welcome the opportunity to show disdain for material concerns ("Occupational Safety and Health Administration," in *Politics of Regulation*, ed. Wilson, p. 253).

Chapter 5

1. Memorandum from Andrew Adams to John Wodatch, May 7, 1975.

2. The executive order had been interpreted in Circular A-107 of the Office of Management and Budget and in HEW draft guidelines issued on June 23, 1975.

3. Memorandum from Martin Gerry to David Mathews, July 23, 1975.

4. Dave M. O'Neill, "Discrimination Against Disabled Persons: The Costs, Benefits and Inflationary Impact of Implementing Section 504 of the Rehabilitation Act of 1973 Covering

Recipients of HEW Financial Assistance," Feb. 1976, published in *Federal Register*, May 17, 1976, pp. 20312–80.

5.   Ibid., p. 20365.

6.   Until late 1975, there were only ten staff people working under Wodatch on detail from other sections of OCR. The federal fiscal 1976 budget included forty permanent positions for the Office of New Programs, whose sole responsibility was implementing Section 504. At the time of the hearing, only one position beyond the original ten had been filled, with twenty others in the process of being filled and the remainder to be filled by September of 1976.

7.   "Nondiscrimination on the Basis of Handicap," *Federal Register*, May 17, 1976, p. 20296.

8.   419 F. Supp. 922 (D.D.C. 1976).

9.   National Center for Law and the Handicapped, "Comment on Notice of Intent to Issue Proposed Rules," South Bend, Ind., June 15, 1976.

10.   National Association of State Universities and Land-Grant Colleges, "Comment on Notice of Proposed Rulemaking," Washington, D.C., Sept. 20, 1976.

11.   American Council on Education, "Comment on Notice of Proposed Rulemaking," Washington, D.C., Sept. 14, 1976.

12.   These recipients included colleges and universities, and David Mathews was about to resume the presidency of the University of Alabama, a post he had held until he was appointed secretary of HEW.

13.   Letter from David Mathews to Harison A. Williams, Jr., Jan. 18, 1977.

14.   Quoted in a letter from Frank Bowe to President Carter, April 2, 1977.

15.   Libassi, however, did have a child with a learning disability, which gave him some insight into the perspective of individuals with disabilities.

Notes

16. Joseph A. Califano, Jr., *Governing America: An Insider's Report from the White House and the Cabinet* (New York: Simon and Schuster, 1981), p. 261.

17. This account is based largely on a report of the meeting made at the time by Jill Robinson of the National Center for Law and the Handicapped. Robinson's observations were corroborated by Peter Libassi in a personal interview.

18. Edward Koch, while a member of the House of Representatives, was a leading proponent of civil rights for disabled people. Several years later, following his election as mayor of New York City, he became a prominent critic of the accessibility requirements in the Section 504 regulation.

19. Press release, HEW, April 28, 1977.

20. "Nondiscrimination on Basis of Handicap: Programs and Activities Receiving or Benefiting from Federal Financial Assistance," *Federal Register*, May 4, 1977, pp. 22676–702.

21. David Tatel, "Complying with Section 504: The Costs Have Been Exaggerated," press release, HEW, July 29, 1977.

22. Cited in ibid.

Chapter 6

1. There was one highly publicized incident involving the public library in Rudd, Iowa, a small farming community of 429 persons. The Rudd Library was ordered to build a ramp for its front entrance by the Iowa State Library Commission because of Section 504, despite the fact that no one in the town used a wheelchair. The cost of the ramp would have been double the annual operating budget of the library. Members of Congress and the *New York Times* became involved, urging that the federal government either pay for mandated architectural changes or not require them. The Washington office of OCR, caught unaware by the publicity, quickly issued assurances that a ramp would not be necessary in situations such as those of the Rudd Library. Nevertheless, the incident linked Section 504 with the problems of bureaucratic overkill by the federal government in the minds of many people.

2. Cornelia W. Bailey, *The Federal 504 Handicapped Access Regulations: A Case Study in Government–Higher Education Relations* (Cambridge, Mass.: Sloan Commission on Government and Higher Education, Jan. 31, 1979).

3. State vocational rehabilitation agencies had traditionally paid for aids. However, since the implementation of Section 504, many state agencies have refused to pay for some services, stating that colleges and universities are obligated to pay for them under Section 504. Law suits have been filed in several states involving the issue of who should pay for what services. In 1981, ACE asked Vice President Bush's commission on regulatory reform to review the Section 504 regulation's provisions on auxiliary aids. Significantly, this was the only part of the regulation that ACE sought to have reviewed, demonstrating institutional support for Section 504 within higher education.

4. Letter from Senate Subcommittee on the Handicapped to Caspar Weinberger, Nov. 13, 1973.

5. Decision by William P. Gray, *Paralyzed Veterans of America et al. v. William French Smith et al.*, 27 CCH EPD P32, 277 (C.D.Ca. 1981).

6. The Community Services Administration was eliminated by the Reagan administration on October 1, 1981, and its programs were either abolished or transferred to the Department of Health and Human Services.

7. Criticisms of the DOT Section 504 regulation are summarized in Congressional Budget Office, *Urban Transportation for Handicapped Persons: Alternative Federal Approaches* (Washington, D.C.: The Office, Nov. 1979).

8. This position is presented in Frank Bowe, *Access to Transportation* (Washington, D.C.: American Coalition of Citizens with Disabilities, 1980).

9. This standard is explained and defended in U.S. Department of Transportation, *Comments on Transportation for Handicapped Persons* (Washington, D.C.: The Department, June 9, 1980).

Notes

10. *Southeastern Community College v. Davis*, 99 S. Ct. 2361 (June 11, 1979).

Chapter 7

1. Some of the reasons for the success of reformist social movements in the United States are analyzed in William A. Gamson, *The Strategy of Social Protest* (Homewood, Ill.: Dorsey Press, 1975).

2. Both the existing civil rights and rehabilitation statutes had been enacted in the previous decade and the programs were still in the process of being defined. Thus the term orthodoxy must be taken as a relative characterization. Nevertheless, proponents of newly strengthened programs may be all the more protective of their recent gains.

3. A similar analysis was made of the lack of interest group involvement in the reform programs of the early 1960s by Nathan Glazer (cited in Daniel Patrick Moynihan, "The Professionalization of Reform," in *The Great Society Reader*, ed. Marvin E. Gettleman and David Mermelstein [New York: Random House, 1967], p. 463).

4. Another important factor was the series of judicial decisions establishing several rights for disabled people. Several of these decisions are summarized in Chapter 2.

5. It is true that in some situations differential treatment has been sanctioned as a remedy to past discrimination under Title VI and Title IX. However, such remedies are typically justified as temporary adjustments to achieve parity among groups rather than as an intrinsic premise, as in the case of Section 504.

6. For examples of both types of relationships in regulatory agencies, see the case studies presented in *The Politics of Regulation*, ed. James Q. Wilson (New York: Basic Books, 1980).

7. Hugh Heclo, "Issue Networks and the Executive Establishment," in *The New American Political System*, ed.

Anthony King (Washington, D.C.: American Enterprise Institute for Public Policy Research, 1978).

8. Sapir has defined symbols as "elaborate objects and devices . . . which are not ordinarily regarded as important in themselves but which point to ideas and actions of great consequences to society" (Edward Sapir, "Symbolism," in *Encyclopedia of the Social Sciences* 14 [New York, MacMillan, 1934]: 492–95).

9. The role of ideology as a source of cohesion and social control is discussed in Ann Swidler, *Organization Without Authority: Dilemmas of Social Control in Free Schools* (Cambridge, Mass.: Harvard University Press, 1979).

10. Steven Kelman, "Occupational Safety and Health Administration," in *Politics of Regulation*, ed. Wilson, pp. 253–54.

11. James G. March and Herbert A. Simon, *Organizations* (New York: John Wiley and Sons, 1958).

12. Richard Cyert and James G. March, *A Behavioral Theory of the Firm* (Englewood Cliffs, N.J.: Prentice-Hall, 1963); James G. March, "The Technology of Foolishness," in *Organizations of the Future*, ed. Harold Leavitt, Lawrence Pinfield, and Eugene Webb (New York: Praeger Publishers, 1974); Michael D. Cohen and James G. March, *Leadership and Ambiguity: The American College President* (New York: McGraw-Hill, 1974); James G. March and Johan P. Olsen, *Ambiguity and Choice in Organization* (Oslo, Norway: Universitetsforlaget, 1976).

13. For a discussion of how health care crises are created, see Robert R. Alford, *Health Care Politics* (Chicago: University of Chicago Press, 1975).

14. Paul J. Quirk, "Food and Drug Administration," in *Politics of Regulation*, ed. Wilson, pp. 191–235.

15. Harold Seidman, *Politics, Position, and Power: The Dynamics of Federal Organization* (2nd ed.; New York: Oxford University Press, 1975), pp. 34–35.

16. Murray Edelman, *The Symbolic Uses of Politics* (Urbana:

Notes

University of Illinois Press, 1963); Joseph R. Gusfield, *Symbolic Crusade* (Urbana: University of Illinois Press, 1964); Thurman Arnold, *The Folklore of Capitalism* (New Haven, Conn.: Yale University Press, 1937).

Index

Index

Index

Index

198

Index

Index

204